LONDON'S CHURCHES & CATHEDRALS

LONDON'S CHURCHES & CATHEDRALS

Text by
Stephen Humphrey

Photography by
James Morris

Foreword by
Andrew Lloyd Webber

New Holland

CONTENTS

Foreword by Andrew Lloyd Webber

When I was a boy, my first love was art and architecture. My long-suffering parents were forced to spend summer holidays somewhere where there were buildings that I wanted to see.

My poor parents were even coerced one year to rent a house near Port Talbot because I wanted to explore the churches and castles of the Vale of Glamorgan. I mean no disrespect to the vast number of residents of that conurbation who have had the taste to buy this book, when I say that the steelworks in these parts were not the perfect holiday environment for the old flesh and blood.

I was not quite thirteen when I went to Westminster School. The school has the extraordinary good fortune of a special relationship with Westminster Abbey. Of course, those twice-a-day services rubbed off on me. Anyone remotely moved by architecture would be affected by evening prayers in St Faith's chapel, reached by night when I was a kid through the dark, shadow-ridden south transept of London's Gothic masterpiece.

Another great joy of being at school at Westminster was that London's churches were on the doorstep. It was in my teens that I discovered Butterfield's All Saints Margaret Street, where, before I was born, my father was the organist and choirmaster. I shall never forget my first visit to Pearson's St Augustine Kilburn. Both are represented in this book.

In the 1960s, these inner city churches were open to all throughout the day. Come 1990, however, most of them were locked, partly for security reasons and partly, frankly, due to the unwillingness of clergy and parishioners to keep them open: keeping churches open is a hassle.

That's why I founded The Open Churches Trust. Its purpose was to open churches that would otherwise be locked. Over a hundred such buildings were opened by the Trust*.

The Trust was responsible for Celebration 2000, which caused 25,000 churches to open their doors for a Millennium Day service and for church bells to be rung over the length and breadth of Britain.

This book is a splendid record of the ecclesiastical architectural joys to be found in London. I am grateful to the publishers of this excellent tome for their donation to the Open Churches Trust and hope you will enjoy these buildings as much as I have done.

Andrew Lloyd Webber

*N.B. In December 2006, the Open Churches Trust ceased being an active organisation. In its twelve years it transformed attitudes to locked churches and many thousands of places of worship are now open on a regular basis. The list of member churches is maintained on the website: www.openchurchestrust.org.uk.

Introduction

London has grown so considerably in the past century and a half, that it is all but impossible to think of its limited compass when Queen Victoria succeeded to the throne. It seems bizarre to think of Greenwich as a detached town, or of Kilburn as a rural hamlet on the Edgware Road. It is a fact that London was a markedly smaller city in the comparatively recent past. Maps of London published as late as the 18th and early 19th centuries were routinely stated as covering London, Westminster and Southwark, as if no other areas mattered. London was equated with what we now call 'the City', the financial quarter lying east of the centre. This was the original London, the *Londinium* of Roman times, and also the walled city of medieval times. To the west of the walled city, a vigorous trading settlement called *Lundenwic* grew up in the 7th and 8th centuries, which St Bede the Venerable called 'the mart of many nations coming by land and sea'. But the Vikings came in the 9th century and the Londoners retreated within the walls.

Westminster, the suburb further upstream, derived its eminence from its abbey and from its royal palace. The abbey was founded at an unknown date, but probably no later than the reign of King Offa (757–796). It was King Edward the Confessor's establishing a palace nearby and his rebuilding of the abbey as a coronation and royal burial church in the 11th century that confirmed Westminster's importance. Westminster Abbey certainly has the greatest historical resonance of any church in London. The other ancient suburb was Southwark, south of London Bridge. This was a mediaeval town in its own right and had an ancient minster church, which became Southwark Cathedral in the early 20th century. It was in fact the first suburb, for it came into existence as a result of the river crossing in Roman times.

Mediaeval London had a stupendous number of parish churches. There are known to have been at least 110 built in the one square mile of the City alone. Of these, 86 were burnt in the Great Fire of 1666. The riches that were destroyed in terms of buildings, furnishings and monuments are incalculable. The fabrics and contents of two surviving mediaeval churches – St Helen's, Bishopsgate, and St Bartholomew the Great, Smithfield – give an instructive glimpse of the losses in 1666. Only seven mediaeval churches survive in the City, plus a few stray towers. Outside the City, mediaeval survivors are equally rare. Westminster Abbey and Southwark Cathedral are immensely important exceptions, but they were both monastic. Parish churches of mediaeval date are very few. The only mediaeval Anglican parish church in central London outside the City is St Margaret's, Westminster, which is a representative of the last architectural style of the Middle Ages. The much-restored St Etheldreda's at Holborn Circus, together with the chapel of Lambeth Palace and the

ABOVE LEFT Sir Ninian Comper's chancel screen at St Cyprian's, Clarence Gate is a fine Edwardian version of a 15th-century style.

OPPOSITE The interior of the Church of St Mary Abbots, Kensington.

undercroft of St Stephen's chapel in the Palace of Westminster, are all survivors of two-storey mediaeval private and institutional chapels. The chapel at Lambeth is Early English, while St Etheldreda's and St Stephen's are early Decorated. Beyond these buildings in central London, the church tourist has to go as far as St Dunstan's, Stepney, to see a complete mediaeval church. The Great Fire and the pressure to rebuild older churches in Georgian and Victorian times made London unusual in having so few mediaeval churches and conversely in having so notable a concentration of churches of the first importance built from the 17th to the 19th centuries. The contrast with counties such as Norfolk and Somerset is therefore considerable.

Why did mediaeval London have so many churches? The question may be asked of most old English cities – Norwich, York, Winchester – and the answer is the same in all cases, namely, that churches were founded by laypeople to serve their own small districts, and not by bishops, who would have imposed a pattern of far fewer but possibly grander churches. Salisbury is an exceptional 'bishop's city' in that sense, but most English cities in the Middle Ages had a patchwork of often tiny parishes. By the end of the 12th century their boundaries were established, and after that time there were few alterations until the 16th-century Reformation.

The earliest churches in London were probably founded in the early 7th century. St Paul's Cathedral was certainly founded in 604. The earliest surviving fabric in a London church is at All Hallows by the Tower, where an arch could be part of a church associated with St Erkenwald, Bishop of London, in the late 7th century. Otherwise, it is the Norman age, in the 11th and 12th centuries, that offers the earliest churches. St John's Chapel in the Tower of London, which is so often overlooked as it is not a parish church, is a complete church of the late 11th century – a rarity anywhere – and an original part of William the Conqueror's Tower. Another non-parochial building, the Temple Church, is a 12th-century Norman round

church, the only one in London and one of only four left in England, which had the honour of consecration by the Patriarch of Jerusalem in 1185. Its later aisled chancel is a foremost example of 13th-century Early English work. The final Norman church is St. Bartholomew the Great at Smithfield: although it is much restored, it nevertheless affords a good instance of the ponderous grandeur of 12th-century design.

The average mediaeval church was enlarged and remodelled on many occasions: a new chapel would be added, new parapets, a further stage on top of the tower. In England generally, the 15th and early 16th centuries were notable for such enlargements and for many spectacular new churches. Central London's examples are St Giles's at Cripplegate (now the Barbican's parish church), St Andrew Undershaft, St Olave's in Hart Street and St Margaret's at Westminster. They have all faced much restoration but their late mediaeval architecture still stands out. After their construction, the Reformation occurred and very little church-building took place between the mid-16th century and the Great Fire. The churches that were built in that period are nevertheless very interesting. St Katharine Cree in the City (built 1628–31) is a curious hybrid of Gothic and Classical styles, and had a connection with William Laud when he was the Bishop of London. At almost the same time, however, the first wholehearted English Classicist, Inigo Jones, was building St Paul's at Covent Garden (1631–3) for the Earl of Bedford's 'piazza', and he had already completed the Queen's Chapel at St James's Palace (1623–7): the latter deserves

notice as the first wholly Classical church in London. It must have seemed as extraordinary at the time as Jones's Banqueting House in Whitehall. The contemporary chapel of Lincoln's Inn, on the other hand, was still wholly Gothic.

Following the Great Fire, Rebuilding Acts in 1667 and 1670 determined work on the City churches for almost half a century. Sir Christopher Wren was appointed to head a commission, whose task was to rebuild 51 of the 86 burnt City churches (in addition to rebuilding St Paul's Cathedral). Wren himself was the architect of such prominent parish churches as St Stephen's, Walbrook, and St Mary-le-Bow in Cheapside, but it has been argued that Wren's fellow-surveyors, Robert Hooke and Nicholas Hawksmoor, also had major parts in the overall scheme. It has also become more apparent in recent years that mediaeval fabric was retained in a number of churches after the Great Fire. The churches kept their old sites but they were rebuilt to all manner of ground-plans. In contrast to their mediaeval predecessors, many of them were given centralizing plans, that is, with an emphasis on the crossing, generally by the arrangement of columns and sometimes by adding a dome. But in all Wren's churches, the altar was kept at the east end and its reredos or screen of honour was the greatest furnishing. The dark-stained woodwork of a Wren church, consisting of pews, pulpit and tester, door-cases, wainscot, galleries and reredos, is one of the glories of the City. The church of St Magnus the Martyr in Lower Thames Street provides a good example; the domed St Mary Abchurch is another.

Victorian redevelopment and the Second World War have reduced Wren's legacy, but the City still possesses much that is of the first importance in church fabric from Wren's time.

St Paul's Cathedral and the City churches were rebuilt from the proceeds of a tax on coal brought into London. By the early 1700s, when the rebuilding after the Great Fire was coming to an end, parishes outside the City looked to the coal tax as a benevolence that might be extended to them. St Mary's at Rotherhithe, for instance, whose parish was known for its maritime connections, had an attractive argument: as the parish's many mariners were prominent in bringing the coal to London and so in providing the income, would it not be fair to use some of the money to rebuild St Mary's? Parliament decided against Rotherhithe, but another petition in 1711 from St Alfege's, Greenwich, had a more favourable and quite remarkable response. The government was prompted to pass into law the Fifty New Churches Act.

This extraordinary event was prompted, of course, by more than St Alfege's petition. The government wished to strengthen the Anglican Church in London and to give prominence to its religious preferences in what it saw as a rising tide of Non-conformity. New churches were essential if the Church of England was to keep up with London's expansion. The Act specified that St Alfege's was to be rebuilt, and also reserved some money for Westminster Abbey and Greenwich Hospital, but further decisions were left to the newly appointed Commissioners. Among them was the elderly Sir Christopher Wren. He made recommendations for the proposed churches, which are often quoted but are naturally thought to be connected to his own City churches in an earlier generation. In fact, they were prompted by the Act of 1711. The Commissioners initially decided that all the new churches were to be built of stone in prominent positions, and that they would possess steeples and porticoes. More remarkably, given that the Act produced such varied churches, the Commissioners determined at the beginning to build all their churches to the same design. It was not long before this decision was forgotten (to London's great benefit). The discussions over the sites for the new churches and their designs were often protracted.

Designs came in from the Commissioners' surveyors (Hawksmoor and William Dickinson at the beginning, then James Gibbs, and afterwards John James), and from some of the Commissioners themselves. As it was, the churches that were built were monumental Baroque works. Twelve complete churches were built, of which six were by Hawksmoor alone and two more were by Hawksmoor in collaboration with John James. Hawksmoor's Christ Church at Spitalfields, St George's in Bloomsbury and St Anne's at Limehouse are all among London's most important churches. These and the other 1711 Act churches show a marked concern with centralizing plans, but as in Wren's buildings, the altar at the east end still imposed an east–west emphasis. The exteriors of the churches of 1711 are more exuberant than Wren's, however, with porticoes and doorways far

more dramatic than Wren provided, other than at St Paul's Cathedral. Hawksmoor's distinctive spirit was matched by Thomas Archer at St John's, Smith Square, and at St Paul's, Deptford. Gibbs and James were more subdued in their designs, making themselves heirs of the Wren tradition.

The great works of the Act came to an end in the 1730s. Nevertheless, many churches were rebuilt in the 18th century: on the fringes of the City, at Shoreditch, Hackney, Clerkenwell and Paddington. They tended to be in the tradition of Wren and Gibbs rather than in the grander 1711 image.

The 19th century brought more church-building to London than all the previous Christian centuries put together. This was partly a matter of trying to keep pace with the rise in population, and partly a matter of new energies and procedures in the Church itself. In Georgian times, an Anglican parish was also what we would call a borough: its vestry or parish council was the equivalent of a borough council. So a new parish brought a new borough into being, and required parliamentary sanction. This was changed in early Victorian times, and the Church could then set up a new parish without the complications of civil government. Above all, in 19th-century England there was a tremendous driving force in the Church to expand its work, for there was a sense that the new industrial towns might be lost to Christianity if efforts were not made (or possibly, from the Anglican viewpoint, they would be lost to Methodism or the Baptists). There was a new urgency and energy in all parts of the Church. Theological colleges, schools, training colleges for

teachers, missions, almshouses, hospitals and monasteries were all founded in some numbers under Church auspices in Victorian times. Church buildings themselves appeared by the hundred. The first great wave of church-building in 19th-century London was under parliamentary authority, as in 1711. In 1818 and again in 1824, parliamentary grants were made for new churches, and a body known as the Church Building Commissioners was set up. Whereas a dozen new churches resulted from the 1711 Act, several hundred were built after 1818. Many were brick-built in a simple Perpendicular style, which do not stand out, but in the 1820s some were grand Greek Revival buildings such as St John's, Waterloo, and St George's, Camberwell. The grandest of all in this category, though not built by the Commissioners, was St Pancras New Church, designed by the Inwoods.

The Classical gave way to the Gothic in the next twenty or thirty years. A. W. N. Pugin, the great proponent of Gothic, wrote his polemic books in the 1830s and 1840s. He called Gothic the only Christian style. To him, Greek Revival buildings were pagan. He contributed St George's Cathedral himself as an exemplar, which was also, incidentally, one of a number of new Roman Catholic churches that appeared in 19th-century London. Until the end of the previous century, they would have been illegal. In the 19th century, newly freed from restrictions, the Roman Catholics built grandly – most obviously at Brompton, where the London Oratory was built, and at the end of the century, in the form of Westminster Cathedral at Victoria. The

Free Churches (among them the Baptists, Independents and Methodists) had been at liberty to build since the late 17th century. Wesley's Chapel in City Road had been a Methodist centre since 1739. All these denominations built new churches in Victorian times, very largely in Gothic, but early this century the Methodist Central Hall at Westminster was an unusually grand Classical building on a plan quite unlike that of any earlier church.

By 1850, practically no Classical churches were being built for the Church of England. Georgian ashlar in Classical dress had given way to Victorian ragstone in Gothic guise. By then, parliamentary grants for church-building were a thing of the past. The Church of England set up its own funds, masterminded by energetic bishops and drawing on the wealth and religious feeling of Victorian England. Bishop Blomfield set up the Metropolis New Churches Fund; his successor as Bishop of London, A. C. Tait, founded the Bishop of London's Fund. South of the river, in the ancient Diocese of Winchester, there was founded the Southwark Fund for Schools and Churches. There were also local building plans such as the Haggerston Church Scheme. At the lowest level, there were innumerable projects to build new churches, sometimes because of a fire (St Giles, Camberwell), or because an old church was considered too small or unfashionable (St Mary Abbots at Kensington and St Matthew's at Bayswater), or because of a memorial gift (St James the Less, Pimlico), or finally because a priest had carved out a mission district for himself to set up a new parish (St Cyprian's,

Clarence Gate). In many cases of rebuilding, there was a sense of producing a church better suited for a prosperous new suburb, in contrast to the small and rustic church it was replacing. St Mary's New Church at Stoke Newington (by Sir Gilbert Scott in 1855–8), which stands opposite the old church it superseded, perfectly illustrates this process. Many Victorian churches in London are unexceptional, but some were markedly important: models for their age. This was intended from the beginning at All Saints, Margaret Street (1850–9), but it was also true in varying ways for Sir Gilbert Scott's churches at Camberwell and Kensington, and for Comper's St Cyprian's, Clarence Gate (1902–3).

The population increases in central London and the nearest suburbs, which prompted the Victorians to build so substantially, were followed by equally drastic decreases in the 20th century. The old Borough of Finsbury, for example, had 153,000 people in 1861, but only 35,000 by 1951. The Second World War brought a huge decrease. Churches began to be demolished because of lack of need. Bombs destroyed many more, and in the less generous post-war years, the Victorian legacy has been greatly reduced. Most of the older churches that were bombed were restored by the 1960s, albeit on new lines in many cases: Most Holy Trinity Church at Dockhead, Bermondsey, was built anew by H. S. Goodhart-Rendel in striking neo-Norman form.

Our inheritance of churches cannot be taken for granted. In 1988, the Wren church of St Mary-at-Hill was burnt, and in 1993 the mediaeval St Ethelburga's in Bishopsgate was largely destroyed by an IRA bomb. Restorations are under way in both cases, but much will still have been lost. A completely new church was built for the parish of St Barnabas, Dulwich, after a fire in 1992: a very rare example of a wholly new church built so near the centre of London in the last quarter of a century.

Much was made in the 1950s and 1960s of new ground-plans for churches, to accommodate changing liturgical trends. In fact, almost all the plans had been tried somewhere before, often many centuries earlier, but what was new was the gauntness and starkness of the outer shell. No previous generation had built so meanly and so bereft of decoration. The tide has now turned, and more traditional ideas have resurfaced. The rebuilding of St. Ethelburga's in the City will possibly be a reflection of these changes. Mediaeval London will still be pointing the way for church-builders today.

N.B. Author's Conventions for Churches

In this book, a capital C has been used for chapel when it is a separate building (e.g. Wesley's Chapel) but a lower case c when it is a subsidiary part of a church (e.g. the Lady chapel of Westminster Cathedral). A capital C for church refers to a building's formal title – St Margaret's Church, Westminster – or to the body of believers as a whole ('The Church in Victorian London...'). The cardinal directions are given in their liturgical sense and not their geographical reality. Although a few churches do not face east, the high altar is always taken to be at the east end, and the other directions follow.

Locations

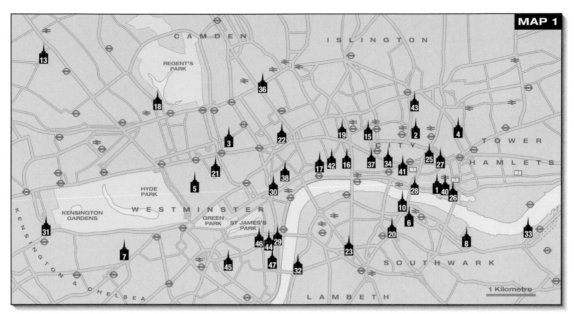

MAP 1

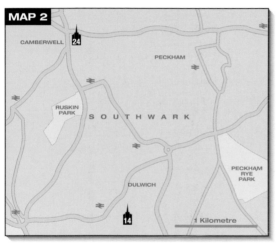

MAP 2

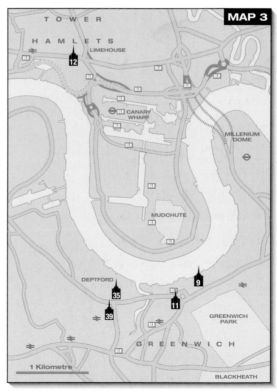

MAP 3

St Paul's Cathedral

Ludgate Hill

HISTORY

- Built in 1675–1710 by Sir Christopher Wren after the Great Fire
- Stands on the site of previous cathedral churches of the Diocese of London back to 604
- Burial place of Viscount Nelson and the Duke of Wellington, and of Wren himself

OF SPECIAL INTEREST

- The inner dome and its decorations and 'whispering gallery'
- The memorial to John Donne in the south choir aisle
- The post-war baldacchino over the high altar, by S. E. Dykes Bower
- The Duke of Wellington's monument under an arch on the north side of the nave, and his tomb in the crypt
- The monument to Nelson in the south transept, and his tomb in the crypt under the dome
- Choir-stalls by Grinling Gibbons and screens in the choir by Jean Tijou
- Holman Hunt's painting *The Light of the World* in the north transept

ABOVE The inner dome painted in monochrome.

OPPOSITE The dome and lantern rise above the north-west tower and the west portico; on the apex of the latter's pediment stands St Paul.

'Reader, if you seek a monument, look around you', translates the inscription above Sir Christopher Wren's tomb in St Paul's Cathedral. It is the most celebrated epitaph in London, for it refers so simply to the prodigious achievement of designing London's cathedral and of seeing it built from start to finish within one lifetime. St Paul's was rebuilt by Wren between 1675 and 1710, and it so happens that one Bishop of London – Henry Compton – was in office throughout those years. The great building was erected to house his throne or *cathedra*, the symbol of his authority as a teacher of the Christian faith.

Wren was given the opportunity to rebuild St Paul's when the mediaeval building was destroyed in the Great Fire. But he was involved in plans for its reconstruction before 1666. The cathedral had suffered depredations in Cromwell's time and it was gradually decaying because of mediaeval structural deficiencies. Wren was first called in to advise on its restoration in 1663. His architectural career had only just begun at that time, although two years earlier King Charles II had invited him to supervise the fortification of Tangier. Wren was always to have King Charles's support and confidence, and it is much to the Merry Monarch's credit that he should have been on amiable terms with such a competent worthy as Wren.

Wren proposed the building of a dome for Old St Paul's early in 1666, but the Great Fire intervened. A completely new building was soon considered necessary. Wren soon became central to the plan for rebuilding. Dean Sancroft wrote to him in 1668: '...you are so absolutely and indispensably necessary to us, that we can do nothing, resolve on nothing without you'. Wren's first design was produced in 1669, but was considered too drastic a change from inherited mediaeval convention. It was superseded by the design of the Great Model of 1673, which was a domed Greek cross. This, too, was well out of step with tradition. A third design, known as the Warrant Design, received a royal warrant in 1675; it was longitudinal, but kept a dome over the crossing. The foundation stone was laid on 21 June 1675, when an old memorial stone inscribed with the word *RESURGAM* ('I shall rise

a complex arrangement of lesser arches and balconies. The choir repeats the pattern of the nave, but ends in an apse. There is a clear view to the high altar, over which rises an Italian marble baldacchino by S. E. Dykes Bower, 1958, which replaced a reredos destroyed in the Blitz. It is artistically appropriate and of sufficient size to be the focus of Wren's interior.

The great pulpit on the south-east of the crossing was designed by Lord Mottistone in 1960: an exuberant essay in the Wren style, but with a much larger and heavier tester than we see in the City's parish churches. The traditional eagle lectern to the west of the crossing is by Jacob Sutton, 1720. The four statues in the angles between the aisles form a set agreed by the Dean and Chapter in the 1790s. John Flaxman executed the statue of Dr Johnson in the north-east corner; the rest (of John Howard, Sir William Jones and Sir Joshua Reynolds, in clockwise order) were by John Bacon the elder. Two of the finest craftsmen associated with Wren

carried out distinguished works in the choir and its aisles: Jean Tijou, who designed the gates and screens at the west ends of the choir aisles, and north and south of the sanctuary; and Grinling Gibbons, who was responsible for the choir-stalls. The large oval font made of Carrara marble by Francis Bird, 1727, stands at the west end of the nave. Nearby there may be seen *The Light of the World*, which was the third version of this well-known painting by William Holman Hunt, dating from about 1900.

The paintings and mosaics of the inner dome and the vaults of the choir and its aisles were not completed until the early 1900s. Sir James Thornhill had painted the inner dome in monochrome by 1720, representing eight scenes from the life of St Paul, set under an arcade. Dean Milman began further decoration in the mid-19th century. Alfred Stevens designed four Prophets to be executed in mosaic in the dome's west spandrels, and G. F. Watts was responsible for designing the Evangelists for the east side. The lion's share of decoration,

however, fell to Sir William Richmond, who carried out all the work in the choir and its aisles in 1891–1907. The theme of the choir mosaics is taken from the Benedicite and leads towards the figure of Christ the King in the centre of the apse's vault. The stained-glass windows of the apse, by Brian Thomas, about 1960, are mainly blue and gold, and fit in very well with the ensemble of the choir. The far east end was arranged as an American memorial chapel after the war.

The Great Fire destroyed the monuments of Old St Paul's, except for the celebrated memorial to John Donne (died 1631), Dean and poet, which is placed in the south choir aisle. This very moving sculpture by Nicholas Stone shows Donne in his burial shroud. Until the end of the 18th century, Wren's St Paul's possessed no grand monuments. Subsequently, over a period of about 100 years, no fewer than 33 monuments were erected by parliamentary vote. The majority were of heroes of the Napoleonic Wars. Viscount Nelson has a substantial memorial in the south transept, by John Flaxman. A convincing statue is accompanied by an anchor, a lion and Britannia, who is telling two boys of Nelson's victories. Most of the Napoleonic monuments follow the same pattern, with anchors or cannons, lions, figures of history or victory, and a eulogy that centres on the subject's battles. With Nelson in the south transept are Admiral Earl Howe (by Flaxman); General Lord Heathfield (by John Charles Felix Rossi); and Admiral Lord Collingwood (by Richard Westmacott). Sir Thomas Picton, who was killed at Waterloo, is in the north transept; and Viscount Duncan, the victor of Camperdown, and Earl St Vincent, the victor of the Battle of Cape St Vincent, are both in the crypt. The largest Napoleonic monument, to the Duke of Wellington, was not ready until 1877. Alfred Stevens was the sculptor. He was commissioned in 1856 and was sacked in 1870; his chief government tormentor ended up as a representation of Falsehood. The work is an architectural one and harks back to the big canopied memorials of Elizabethan and Jacobean times in Westminster Abbey.

Nelson's tomb lies in the crypt directly under the dome: the greatest place of honour. He was accorded the black marble sarcophagus that Benedetto da Rovezzano had made in the 1520s for Cardinal Wolsey. The tomb is surrounded by memorials to later admirals. In a similar fashion, Wellington's plain granite tomb under the west part of the choir is surrounded by 20th-century soldiers' memorials. Wren's tomb is in the south-east corner. Victorian military heroes are commemorated on the north side of the nave. Kitchener's marble effigy in All Souls' chapel, by Sir William Reid Dick, 1925, is particularly fine, especially as it is part of a memorial chapel of the same era (by Detmar Blow and Sir Mervyn Macartney). In the centre at the west end, a tablet in the floor recalls the St Paul's Watch, whose members helped to save the cathedral during the Second World War.

The cathedral was at a low ebb for much of the 19th century. Stirrings of reform came under Dean Milman (1849–68), but it was Robert Gregory (Canon from 1868, Dean 1891–1911) who was the most celebrated reformer. In his time, St Paul's was hugely raised in influence and esteem. Great state occasions such as the thanksgiving in 1872 for the Prince of Wales's recovery from illness were subsequently to be held there. In more recent memory, there has been the state funeral of Sir Winston Churchill in 1965, an occasion when the world was taken into Wren's masterpiece, thanks to television.

All Hallows by the Tower

Byward Street

HISTORY

- Remodelled in 1948–57 by Lord Mottistone and Paul Paget after wartime bombing
- The mediaeval church was possibly founded as early as the late 7th century
- William Penn, the founder of Pennsylvania, was baptized here in 1644
- Pepys climbed the tower to see the Great Fire in 1666
- Toc H became based in the church when 'Tubby' Clayton became Vicar in 1922

OF SPECIAL INTEREST

- Arch built of Roman tiles that could date from the late 7th century
- Font cover by Grinling Gibbons, 1682
- Toc H Lamp of Maintenance on the Croke tomb

The oldest standing fabric of any London church is to be found at All Hallows'. A tall, narrow arch built of 'recycled' Roman tiles in the south-west corner could be part of a 7th-century church belonging to the great abbey at Barking, miles away across the Essex creeks and marshes. The church has therefore also been known for centuries as All Hallows Barking.

The church has a prominent green copper-covered spire that was built after the Second World War by Lord Mottistone, which surmounts a brick tower of 1658–9 by Samuel Twyne. It was this tower that Samuel Pepys climbed to watch the Great Fire in September 1666 ('up to the top of Barking steeple', where he 'became afeard to stay there long and down again as fast as I could'). Fortunately, the church survived the Great Fire but it was not so lucky in 1940, for the bombing left only the tower, the aisle walls, the north porch, the crypts and various furnishings. These were incorporated in the church that Lord Mottistone and Paul Paget built between 1948 and 1957. They

ABOVE The font cover was carved in limewood by Grinling Gibbons in 1682 to represent three putti holding fruit and flowers.

RIGHT This arch built of reused Roman tiles might date back to the late 7th century.

introduced Gothic arcades of Painswick stone and reinforced concrete roofs, which blend well with the unplastered mediaeval aisle walls.

The most celebrated furnishing is the font cover of 1682, which Grinling Gibbons carved in limewood. Three putti hold fruit and flowers on a circular base, with a dove perched above. An equally well-known fitting from the 20th century is the Toc H Lamp of Maintenance, which stands on the tomb of Alderman John Croke in the north or Toc H chapel. The Reverend P. B. (or 'Tubby') Clayton, who became Vicar in 1922, had run a wartime mission near Ypres called Talbot House, which was translated in signallers' code as 'Toc H'. The arms of Ypres appear over the north porch. The other prominent monument on the south side is an effigy of Alfred Henry Forster by Cecil Thomas, 1919.

No fewer than 17 brasses survive from between 1389 and 1651. The finest commemorates Andrew Evyngar and his wife Ellyn. It dates from about 1533 and is of Flemish workmanship. The church has a pulpit of Wren's time, brought from St Swithin's, London Stone, and three 18th-century sword-rests. The stained glass in the aisle windows is post-war heraldic glass by Reginald Bell and Michael Farrar Bell, chiefly with maritime allusions.

Lancelot Andrewes, the saintly Jacobean Bishop of Winchester, was baptized here in 1555 and called All Hallows' his 'nursing mother' in the faith. Admiral Sir William Penn, who saved the church in 1666 by having houses blown up to create a firebreak, had his son, also William, baptized here in 1644; the son became the founder of Pennsylvania.

All Hallows on the Wall

London Wall

George Dance the younger (1741–1825) built All Hallows' in 1765–7 on the site of a mediaeval church known for its anchorites. Dance's church is in an unusually light Classical style, which marks it out from the generally monumental works of its own century in the City and beyond. The contrast with Hawksmoor's churches is considerable. Dance was only 24 when he designed the church and had studied for six years in Italy; he was strongly influenced by Classical Roman models. All Hallows' is well preserved, despite damage from bombing in 1941, which was not properly remedied until 1960–2, by David Nye. From then until 1994 the church was occupied by the Council for the Care of Churches. All Hallows' is now used by various charities.

The street in which it stands runs along the south side of the line of the City's Roman and mediaeval wall. A stretch of the wall can be seen in the churchyard, west of the church, and the north vestry is semicircular because it sits upon the base of a bastion of the City's wall. All Hallows' has an austere exterior. Its brick-built south elevation has just three large semicircular lunettes high up in the wall. The stone-faced west tower stands forward of the nave and is unremarkable except for its pedimented Tuscan doorway and domed cupola. The cross and ball were added by Sir Arthur Blomfield in 1898 on the model of St Paul's Cathedral for Samuel John Stone, Rector.

The interior is a surprise after the plain exterior. It is aisleless and is structurally undivided. Thin, fluted Ionic columns stand against the side walls and mark out three principal bays. There is a light frieze that runs round the church, but no cornice. The columns appear at first glance to support arcades, because the arches of the lunettes and their indentations into the barrel-vault seem to rest on them. The vault has shallow coffering. The chancel is marked out by a low wooden screen of 1962, which can be raised if required. The pulpit stands against the north wall and can be entered only from the vestry. It is a three-decker that has lost its lowest deck. The pews have been removed, but choir-stalls remain. The west gallery, which rests on Tuscan columns, houses the organ.

OPPOSITE Fluted Ionic columns articulate this light Classical interior by George Dance the younger. The coffered apse houses a painting of Ananias restoring St Paul's sight.

St Bartholomew the Great

West Smithfield

HISTORY

- Norman priory church founded in the early 12th century by Rahere, a courtier of King Henry I
- Belonged to the Augustinian Order in the Middle Ages
- Hogarth was baptized here in 1697
- Extensively restored by Sir Aston Webb from 1884

OF SPECIAL INTEREST

- Half-timbered Tudor gatehouse
- Ponderous Norman nave
- 12th-century pointed crossing arches
- 15th-century monument to Rahere
- Prior Bolton's oriel window in the nave
- Tudor and Stuart monuments

OPPOSITE The 15th-century monument to Rahere, the founder, occupies the traditional place of honour on the north side of the sanctuary.

The mediaeval City of London had many monasteries, but this is the only major one whose church survives, and moreover the greater part of the standing fabric is Norman. The Priory and Hospital of St Bartholomew were founded in the early 12th century by Rahere, a prebendary of St Paul's and a courtier of King Henry I, after he had recovered from a life-threatening illness on a visit to Rome. When the priory was dissolved in 1539, the east part of its church was retained as a parish church, and the nave was demolished to provide space for a churchyard. In the 19th and early 20th centuries much restoration took place here, especially under Sir Aston Webb from 1884 onwards, but also including the rebuilding of the visually important east apse in 1864–6 under William Slater and T. Hayter Lewis. The good internal stonework of the restoration contrasts with the flints that were used externally. Webb was the churchwarden's brother, which explains his involvement in a parish church, when he is otherwise associated with big secular buildings such as Buckingham Palace. The heavy solemnity of the Norman work combines with the darkness of the interior to produce a monumental and antique atmosphere that is unlike that of any other City church.

The church is reached from West Smithfield through a 13th-century gateway that supports a half-timbered building of 1595. A statue of Rahere fixed to this building was given by Sir Aston Webb in 1917. The gateway once led into the mediaeval south nave aisle. Its date is indicated by the dog-tooth moulding, which is a badge of the 13th-century Early English style. The path through the churchyard leads to Webb's two-storey porch of 1893 and to a 17th-century brick tower, which is plain, apart from battlements and a cupola. Across the churchyard to the right there is the restored east walk of the priory's cloister. The 12th-century entrance to it is seen on the right immediately after entering the church. The cloister was recovered for church use in two stages in the early 20th century.

The interior consists of the four-bay mediaeval choir, with an apse, choir aisles that run round the apse to form an ambulatory, a Lady chapel

+ hic jacet Raherus Primus Canonicus et Primus Prior hujus Ecclesiæ

BELOW LEFT *The 13th-century doorway viewed from West Smithfield is surmounted by a half-timbered building of 1595 that bears a statue of Rahere, the Norman founder of St Bartholomew's Priory and Hospital.*

BELOW RIGHT *Prior William Bolton's oriel window bears his symbol of a crossbow bolt shot through a barrel or tun.*

ABOVE RIGHT *The heavy Norman piers march round the east end of the mediaeval choir.*

BELOW RIGHT *The ambulatory forms a processional way round the mediaeval east end.*

to the east, transepts, and one bay of the nave. The choir is the dominant part. It consists of heavy circular piers with scalloped capitals; arches that are plain except for an outer frame of billet decoration; a gallery of four narrow arched openings per bay under a blind arch; and, finally, a much lighter 14th-century clerestory. The transepts are substantially 19th century (and only half as deep as their predecessors), as is the Lady chapel, which was originally completed in 1336. Notice that the north and south arches of the crossing are pointed, despite retaining their Norman shafts. Here we have an early use of the pointed arch in the 12th century, even earlier, it seems, than that at the Temple Church. The only further structural feature of interest is the oriel window on the south side of the choir, which was built at gallery level in about 1517 by Prior William Bolton. It has cusped and transomed lights, and bears its builder's symbol, a crossbow *bolt* shot through a barrel or *tun*. The one bay of the nave is preserved

because the mediaeval pulpitum, or screen, at the west end of the area used as the canons' choir once separated it from the rest of the nave.

The furnishings are largely Victorian and early 20th century. Webb designed the agreeable screen to the Lady chapel in 1897, and was responsible for the pulpit and the lectern. The stalls, the west gallery and the organ case also all date from the late 19th century. The font is an exception, for it dates from about 1405, which appears to make it the only mediaeval font in the City. What St Bartholomew's lacks in old furnishings, it makes up for in monuments, which are earlier than usual and are notably numerous from Tudor and Stuart times. First, however, comes the important mediaeval tomb of Rahere himself. He died in about 1145, but his present monument was erected in the early 15th century, in the traditional place of honour on the north side of the sanctuary. A recumbent effigy lies under a canopy. An angel at his feet holds the priory's arms: two golden leopards with two crowns above.

The church's most interesting historical associations are with William Hogarth, who was baptized here in 1697 and Benjamin Franklin, who worked as a printer in the Lady chapel when parts of the church were in secular use.

St Bride's Fleet Street
Fleet Street

HISTORY

- The parish church of 'the street of ink'
- Built in 1671–8 by Sir Christopher Wren after the Great Fire
- Restored in 1955–7 by W. Godfrey Allen after wartime bombing
- Associations with many famous writers and actors

OF SPECIAL INTEREST

- 'Wedding-cake steeple', 69 metres (226 feet) high, 1701–03
- Postwar reredos in the Wren style
- Coat of Arms of Queen Elizabeth II (a modern example of an old tradition) at the west end
- Display of ancient foundations and the parish's history in the crypt

ABOVE The figures of St Bride and St Paul by David McFall stand on the screens at the west end of the nave. The coat of arms of Queen Elizabeth II may be seen on the wall behind.

OPPOSITE The worthy post-war interior by W. Godfrey Allen focuses on the substantial Classical reredos.

Few churches anywhere can have had so remarkable a roll-call of literary and artistic parishioners as St Bride's, and as Fleet Street was until lately the home of national newspapers, the church was the industry's parish church.

St Bride's was Wren's second most costly church after St Mary-le-Bow. It was rebuilt in 1671–8 after the Great Fire, and the famous 'wedding-cake steeple' was added in 1701–3. Among the tallest of Wren's steeples, it rises to 69 metres (226 feet). A local cook, William Rich, modelled his wedding cakes on the steeple, giving rise to its familiar label. The church was restored by W. Godfrey Allen in 1955–7 after the bombing of 1940. The new interior is a worthy Classical design, but it differs considerably from a normal Wren church. The seating is arranged in collegiate style and is all lightly stained, with wide, uncluttered aisles. Wren divided the interior into five bays with paired Tuscan columns, which support block entablatures and coffered arches. Substantial open screens stand in front of the arcades and form the background to the collegiate seating. The nave is barrel-vaulted, with deep splays formed by the oval clerestory windows. The nave focuses on a remarkable reredos, which stands away from the east end and is tall enough to hide all but the top of the east window. Pairs of Corinthian columns support a segmental pediment surmounted by flambeaux. The reredos incorporates an oval stained-glass panel of Christ in glory, by Glyn Jones. Jones also painted the east end behind the reredos in *trompe l'oeil* to suggest an apse. Two charity schoolchildren from the early 18th century stand in the south-west corner. Near them is the font, with a diminutive post-war cover based on Wren's first design for the steeple.

Before W. Godfrey Allen rebuilt the church, Professor W. F. Grimes excavated the ruins. He found the remains of a series of churches going back to a pre-Conquest building of unknown date. There has been speculation that it goes back to the 6th century and was named at once after St Bridget of Kildare, who lived at that time, but such a dedication at so early a date is improbable. The walls found in the excavations, together with a good display on the history of the parish, may be seen in the crypt.

St Helen's Bishopsgate

Great St Helen's

HISTORY

- Survivor of the Great Fire
- Two parallel mediaeval naves, one of which belonged to a Benedictine nunnery
- Restored and reordered by Quinlan Terry after damage by IRA bombs in 1992–3
- Huge array of mediaeval and later monuments

OF SPECIAL INTEREST

- Monument to Sir John Crosby
- Monument to Sir Thomas Gresham, founder of the Royal Exchange (east end)
- Monument to Sir Julius Caesar Adelmare in the south transept
- Jacobean pulpit against the south wall
- Inscribed south doorway of 1633
- Wooden sword-rest of 1665

ABOVE RIGHT The church's oldest monument, to John de Oteswich and his wife, 14th century.

OPPOSITE A view towards the south transept from the parochial choir, over the monument of Sir John Crosby and his wife.

St Helen's is a precious survivor in the City from before the Great Fire and a survivor, too, of modern bomb outrages. It has the best collection of monuments of any parish church in the capital, earning it the label 'the Westminster Abbey of the City'. It is also unusual in its history and ground-plan, for it has two parallel naves, one of which belonged to the mediaeval Benedictine nunnery founded by William Fitzwilliam in the early 13th century. This is the only mediaeval monastic building left within the City's walls and the only one surviving from a nunnery. The nunnery was dedicated to St Helen and the Holy Cross, for St Helen, who was the mother of the first Christian Roman Emperor, Constantine the Great, was widely credited with finding the True Cross in the 4th century.

The church stands in Great St Helen's, off Bishopsgate, largely surrounded by 19th- and 20th-century commercial buildings. They helped to shield its fabric from two IRA bomb blasts in 1992 and 1993, but the first of the bombs nevertheless caused great damage. The church was restored by Quinlan Terry and was considerably reordered. For a City church, St Helen's is fortunate to have a well-supported and successful ministry, which has carried it through its troubles. The visitor approaches a west front of two low, battlemented gables, representing

Quinlan Terry's restoration included the raising of the internal floor. Previously, the entrance was down a flight of steps. A white-painted west gallery has been built across the west end and houses a finely cased organ (by Thomas Griffin, 1743) on the south side. An equally sumptuous doorcase of about 1635, which formerly stood at the main entrance, now stands against the south wall. A second such door-case is placed in the south transept.

There is still a Victorian reredos under the parochial east window, but the focus of the church is the south wall, where the pulpit stands on a dais. The pulpit is a rich Jacobean example, with a tester. The communion table is kept under the east window, but it is moved to the south dais for services. Very little stained glass survived the bombs of 1992–3; what does remain is to be found in the north windows. The middle one depicts Shakespeare, who is recorded as having lived in the parish in 1597. There is also some heraldic glass in the east window on the north side, which was given by the Merchant Taylors' Company in 1996. On the north side of the central arcade there is a rare wooden sword-rest, dated 1665. The font, placed at the west end, was made in 1632.

The most important monuments are at the east end. On the north side there is the tomb-chest of Sir Thomas Gresham (died 1579), founder of the Royal Exchange and of Gresham College and one of the most famous City worthies of all time. The tomb consists of a black marble base, a fluted chest with finely carved heraldry, and a black marble slab on top. Under the arcade to the south of Gresham's monument there is the railed memorial to Sir William

the mediaeval nuns to the north and the parish to the south. A small bell-turret surmounts the centre. The west and north walls, plus the south transept, are 13th century. The windows, however, are from a later period: those at the west are 15th century. The north wall features blocked lancets, which may be seen from inside. The transept's exterior clearly reveals numerous alterations. On that side of the church, too, there is a doorway of 1633, which is inscribed *Laus Deo/S. Helena*.

The interior consists of two naves of equal width, separated by four tall arches of about 1475, and two chancels that are divided by a lower 14th-century arch and then by another arch that dates from the late 15th century. There is no structural division or screenwork on either the north or south side. A screen of 1892–3 by J. L. Pearson, which formerly stood across the parochial chancel, has been moved to fill the arch into the south transept. This transept has an east chapel of the late 14th century; transept and chapel are now treated as one space.

RIGHT *The inscription to Sir John Spencer, Lord Mayor (died 1609), at the west end of the parochial nave.*

BELOW *A view from the east end of the parochial choir towards the nuns' choir, seen through the monument to Sir William Pickering (died 1574).*

Pickering (died 1574), Ambassador to Spain. On the east wall near the arcade is a small monument to Sir Andrew Judd (died 1558), Lord Mayor and founder of Tonbridge School, who went to 'Russia and Muscovy', according to the inscription. The south transept has two large table-tombs. The one on the north is of John de Oteswich and his wife, with effigies from the late 14th century; and the other is of Sir Julius Caesar Adelmare (died 1636), a judge, whose tomb-chest bears not an effigy but a legal document declaring that he was ready to pay the debt of Nature. Under the arch into the transept's aisle is Sir John Crosby's tomb. He was the owner of Crosby Hall, which once stood nearby but is now at Chelsea. He died in 1476. The railed monument under the nave arcade is to William Kirwin (died 1594), a mason, who declares that he has adorned London with buildings. Against the south wall, near the main entrance, Sir John Spencer (died 1609), Lord Mayor, has a substantial wall monument featuring three figures, two coffered arches, black obelisks, strapwork and heraldry.

St Katharine Cree
Leadenhall Street

St Katharine's is in a category by itself, for it was built in 1628–31 in a mixture of Gothic and Classical styles which has no parallel in London's churches. It was built in that brief period when William Laud was the Bishop of London, and when efforts were made to restore and enrich church buildings that had suffered the depredations of the Tudor Reformation. Laud consecrated the church on 31 January 1631.

The church stands at the corner of Leadenhall Street and Creechurch Lane. The south-west tower dates from 1504, except for the uppermost part and for the cupola, which are of 1776. It is tempting to suggest, after a first glance at the church, that it is a building of 1504, remodelled in 1628–31. But the square-headed south windows with cusped lights, which could so easily be late-mediaeval on the basis of those details, have eared labels and distinct aprons or panels beneath them, which could not possibly be of 1504; also, the footings of the earlier aisle wall can be seen. So this amalgam of styles is 17th-century. The only plausible designer so far suggested is Edmund Kinsman.

RIGHT The monument to Sir Nicholas Throckmorton (died 1571) stands above the altar in the Laud chapel. His daughter married Sir Walter Raleigh.

The interior is divided by six-bay arcades of Corinthian columns and coffered round arches that run the length of the church. Gothic returns above the arcades in the form of cusped, three-light clerestory windows, but separated by fluted Corinthian pilasters. At the east end, there is the Gothic form of a rose window set in a square, with five cusped lights below it. Nave and aisles have plaster rib-vaults. The ribs, and the arches and capitals, are all painted blue-grey.

The reredos is a plain, straight-topped Classical example. The mainly yellow stained glass in the rose window is 17th century; that in the five lights below is of 1878 and commemorates the Flower Sermon that was started here in 1853. The communion table and the cedar-wood pulpit are both 18th century. In the south-east corner, there is the Laud chapel, fitted up

ABOVE LEFT The east end of the nave shows the church's mixture of Gothic (in the rose window and the five lights below) and the Classical (in the Corinthian columns and coffered arches).

ABOVE RIGHT The 17th-century font bears the arms of Sir John Gayer.

by the Society of King Charles the Martyr in 1960. A portrait of Archbishop Laud hangs on the east wall. Above the altar in this chapel there is the monument of Sir Nicholas Throckmorton (died 1571), an Elizabethan worthy. He has a recumbent effigy set amidst Classicizing features. The font is original to the church and bears the arms of Sir John Gayer, Lord Mayor, who founded an annual Lion Sermon here in 1649 after escaping from a lion in the Syrian desert.

St Magnus the Martyr

Lower Thames Street

HISTORY

- Built in 1671–6 by Sir Christopher Wren after the Great Fire
- The steeple was added in 1703–6
- Embellished by Martin Travers in the 1920s for Anglo-Catholic worship

OF SPECIAL INTEREST

- Steeple rising to 56 metres (185 feet)
- Projecting clock of 1700 at the west end
- Ornate 17th-century pulpit and tester
- Statue of St Magnus, Earl of Orkney, by Martin Travers
- Model of Old London Bridge

ABOVE The 56-metre steeple of St Magnus the Martyr rises above the surrounding office blocks.

OPPOSITE The reredos of the Lady chapel, made out of a doorcase by Martin Travers, is seen here from the sanctuary, with a statue of Our Lady of Walsingham on the right.

The church stands on the south side of one of the City's busiest roads, a dual carriageway, and in the shadow of Adelaide House, a huge office block of 1921–4. Originally, however, it had a most prominent site, for it stood at the north end of Old London Bridge and appears in numerous Georgian paintings of the river. After the houses and shops had been removed from the bridge in 1760, and the northern approach had been widened, the footway on the downstream side actually went under the church's tower. It is difficult to imagine today that the pavement under the tower was part of such an important route. As L. P. Hartley said, the past is another country. The church existed in William the Conqueror's time in the 11th century and so its patron could not have been the St Magnus who was the Earl of Orkney, for he was not martyred until 1116. Today, the earl is taken to be the patron, as his statue of 1925 in the south aisle by Martin Travers testifies.

Sir Christopher Wren rebuilt the body of the present church in 1671–6 after the Great Fire, and added the steeple in 1703–6. The church was originally of nine bays, of which the central one on the north side survives unaltered with its pedimented doorway, a porthole window and swag decoration. The other windows were once arched, but they were replaced by portholes in 1782. The original west bay, which flanked the tower, was removed in 1762 to allow the footway of the widened bridge to pass under the tower. The visitor who enters by the west door today can see a group of parish boundary marks fixed to the tower. Many such marks still survive in the City. They are chiefly Victorian and indicate parish boundaries from a time when they had a civil as well as an ecclesiastical function.

The steeple rises to 56 metres (185 feet) and is based on that of the church of St Charles Borromée in Antwerp, built by Francis Aiguillon in 1614–24. A short spire sits on a lead dome that in turn surmounts an octagonal lantern. A large clock projecting from the west side was given by Sir Charles Duncombe in 1700. It must have been one of the most familiar clocks in London before 1831, but now it is hidden away behind Adelaide House.

RIGHT *The high altar and reredos make a fine ensemble, consisting of 17th-century work from Wren's time and additions in the same style by Martin Travers in the 1920s. Moses and Aaron flank the altar.*

Entering through a vestibule under the west gallery, the visitor sees an aisled, tunnel-vaulted interior formed by tall Ionic columns with gilded capitals. These are the features that T. S. Eliot famously mentioned in *The Waste Land*. The plan seems longitudinal, but originally there was a wide gap between the columns in line with the north door; in 1924 an additional pair of columns filled that gap and ended the semblance of a crossing. The focus of the interior is the sumptuous reredos, which is double the normal size. The lower part is of Wren's time and the upper part was added in 1924–5 by Martin Travers in a Wren style. The whole is surmounted, unusually, by a rood, which would have offended Protestant susceptibilities in the 17th century but which was a normal badge of the Anglo-Catholic movement of the 1920s, to which St Magnus's was recruited by H. J. Fynes-Clinton (Rector, 1922–59). This is the world of the Anglo-Catholic congresses about which Sir John Betjeman wrote, and which has contributed much to the atmosphere of this church. Fynes-Clinton refounded the Fraternity of Our Lady de Salve Regina, which had existed in the Middle Ages.

Altars are placed diagonally across the south-east and north-east corners, and each has a reredos made from a door-case of Wren's time. The altar to the north serves the Lady chapel; a statue of Our Lady of Walsingham is placed nearby. The pulpit is a fine 17th-century example, with an ornate tester and a notably slender stem. The seating is darkly stained, which accords well with the rest of the furnishings, but it does not consist of box-pews, except for two that have been preserved at the west end. The west gallery houses an organ by Abraham Jordan and his son of the same name, 1712, which was the first to have a swell-box. Charles Duncombe was its donor. Of the seven circular north windows, six contain post-war heraldic glass by Alfred L. Wilkinson; the seventh is 17th-century and came from Plumbers' Hall. The full-length south windows contain glass by Lawrence Lee, including one of St Magnus. At the west end there is a magnificent model of Old London Bridge by David T. Aggett.

South of the high altar there is a tablet to Miles Coverdale, Rector in the 16th century, who translated the Bible into English. Henry Yevele (died 1400), the architect of the naves of Westminster Abbey (see page 52) and Canterbury Cathedral, was buried in the previous church. He was a member of the original Fraternity of Our Lady de Salve Regina.

St Mary-le-Bow

Cheapside

ABOVE Laurence King designed a worthy new interior for St Mary's in 1956–64, within Wren's walls.

FAR RIGHT The steeple was Wren's grandest, rising to 70 metres (230 feet), and still presides over Cheapside as it towered over the City of King Charles II.

Cheapside was the City's main street and market-place ('cheap' or 'chipping' in a place-name refers to a market) and a scene of mediaeval riots. Wren acknowledged its importance by designing for it his grandest steeple. St Mary-le-Bow cost more to rebuild than any other parish church after the Great Fire, and almost half of the money was spent on the steeple. It is a proud structure, 70 metres (230 feet) high and surmounted by a dragon vane 2.7 metres (9 feet) long, which dominates the modern office blocks just as much as it presided over the houses and shops of Restoration London. It stands north of the body of the church, to which it is connected by a vestibule, not merely because it was thereby given a more prominent position, but also because Wren could place better foundations there. George Gwilt the younger restored it and partly rebuilt it in the early 19th century; the dark Aberdeen granite columns below the obelisk are his. It was restored again by Laurence King after wartime bombing. The 12 bells, which the tower holds, the famous 'Bow Bells', are said to define as Cockneys those born within their sound. One of the bells is the Great Bell of Bow, the tenor bell that is the successor of a curfew bell in the Middle Ages. It weighs nearly 2,134 kilograms (42 hundredweight). The peal was last recast in 1956, by the Whitechapel Bell Foundry. The bells are significant not just to Cockneys, but also because the BBC used a recording of them during broadcasts to occupied Europe in the Second World War. As a result, St Mary's has a Norwegian chapel, with a bronze relief by Ragnhild Butenschon, to recall the hope of liberation that Bow Bells brought to wartime Norway.

Wren's church was built in 1671–80. The present church was the work of Laurence King in 1956–64, reusing Wren's walls and steeple. It was a very worthy restoration in Classical style, but it is a distinctive work that differs from a Wren interior. Underneath it there is an 11th-century crypt, which has survived all the surface disasters, the arches or 'bows' of whose vault gave the church its surname and which also named the Church of England's principal court, the Court of Arches. The court has met here over many centuries because it is the court of the Province of

Canterbury, and St Mary's belonged to the Archbishop of Canterbury from early in the Middle Ages; it was described as his main 'peculiar' in London, meaning that it came directly under his jurisdiction and not that of the local bishop, the Bishop of London. Peculiars were once common, for they represented important sources of income. Today, ironically, St Mary's has a bishop's chair in the sanctuary – intended for the Bishop of London.

The body of the church is built in red brick, with Portland stone dressings. The west side now looks onto a small paved square, which centres on a statue of Captain John Smith (died 1631), the founder of Jamestown in Virginia, USA. The nave elevation on this side is surmounted by a pediment that has curved attachments to the aisles. The west doorway in the centre has its own segmented pediment with large brackets.

The barrel-vaulted interior is only three bays long, but it is wide, and because the aisles are so narrow, it seems very spacious. The arcades are supported on square piers, to which Corinthian demi-columns with gilded capitals are attached. There are small chapels at the east ends of the aisles, enclosed with fine iron screens by Grundy Arnatt Ltd: the Norwegian chapel is on the north side, and the Blessed Sacrament chapel on the south. The latter is graced by a tall sacrament house, over which presides a 'pelican in her piety', symbolic of the Eucharist: an excellent modern work, no doubt prompted by the steeple. The bishop's chair now stands north of the sanctuary, but it was intended to stand against the east wall, as in ancient times. What

appears to be the reredos was meant to be a screen of honour for the chair and not a normal altarpiece; a bishop's mitre and the arms of the Bishop of London surmount it. The architecture, however, gives further prominence to the east end, for there are two attached Corinthian columns – as high as those of the arcades – which support block entablatures and, above them, tall pedestals and urns. They give dignity to the focus of the interior. The sanctuary is raised on a step and above it hangs a huge rood, designed by John Hayward and carved at Oberammergau. The stained glass is also by Hayward. It adds to the colour of the church, but it is jagged in design and difficult to follow. Christ in Majesty is in the centre. On the left, the Virgin Mary holds a model of Bow Church surrounded by other City steeples. In the south-west corner, there are two items of Australian interest. One is a bronze bust of Admiral Arthur Philip (died 1814), who led the first settlement at Sydney in 1788; the other is a banner of the Order of Australia, placed here in 1990.

St Stephen Walbrook

Walbrook

HISTORY

- Built in 1672–80 by Sir Christopher Wren after the Great Fire
- The steeple was added in 1713–17
- Significant for its domed interior
- The Samaritans were founded by the Rector in 1954
- Restored by Robert Potter in 1978–87

OF SPECIAL INTEREST

- Fine 17th-century reredos, pulpit and door-case
- Collection of Georgian and Victorian wall memorials
- Marble altar by Henry Moore under the dome

Wren's most remarkable parish church was built in 1672–80, with the steeple added in 1713–17. The exterior is to a large extent hidden behind the Mansion House and is markedly plain. Only the steeple deserves notice. To the south of the tower a door beneath a garlanded oval window leads up a flight of steps into a west apse, which is screened from the interior proper by a substantial door-case.

Wren's plan is formed by the positioning of 16 Corinthian columns of equal height. On the west side, eight of them appear to form a groined nave, flanked by flat-ceilinged inner aisles and narrower outer aisles. But if the first four columns abreast are discounted, the remaining 12 form a centralizing plan in four groups of three in the corners of the square, over which presides a coffered dome of wood and plaster. The groups of columns define an inner square, which is emphasized by the entablature

ABOVE Much of the exterior of St Stephen Walbrook is hidden, but the steeple stands out.

RIGHT Wren's coffered dome sits on eight arches, which are supported by groups of Corinthian columns.

they carry, but they also form a Greek cross out of the transepts, the nave and the chancel. The inner square becomes an octagon by the device of throwing arches across the corners as well as over the arms of the Greek cross, and on these eight arches the dome and its lantern rest. To set against these centralizing features, the arched east window almost fills the chancel wall and there is a substantial reredos at the east end. In recent years, this reredos has lost its role because a central altar has been placed under the dome. This altar was made by Henry Moore of light-coloured marble, is 2.4 metres (8 feet) wide and weighs 8½ tons. Light-coloured benches curve round it. It is incongruous in Wren's church, which needs its altar in front of the reredos; however much Wren's ground-plans set up a tension between longitudinal and centralizing features, the east end was ultimately the focus. The body of the church was intended for high box-pews; without them, the high bases of the columns have lost their purpose.

Robert Potter carried out a major restoration in 1978–87, which has left the church in a remarkably fine condition. Thomas Creecher made the reredos, and William Newman was reponsible for the carving. They also worked together on the fine pulpit and its tester, and Newman carved the font-cover. The organ above the south door was built by William Hill in 1906, but has a case of 1765. One well-known individual who has no memorial here, despite being buried in the north aisle, is Sir John Vanbrugh, the architect of Blenheim Palace and Castle Howard. An epitaph was suggested for him: 'Lie heavy on him, Earth! for he/Laid many a heavy load on thee'.

Temple Church
Fleet Street

A midst the lanes and courtyards of the Inner and Middle Temple, between Fleet Street and the Thames, there is a historical gem: the Temple Church, a rare surviving example of a Norman round church, which was consecrated by Heraclius, Patriarch of Jerusalem, in 1185. It also possesses a distinguished Early English chancel, which is an even more exceptional survival for central London, and it has an interesting collection of mediaeval effigies. The church serves the lawyers of the Middle and Inner Temple, the remote successors of the Knights Templar, whose order was founded to protect pilgrims in the Holy Land. The capture of Jerusalem in the First Crusade led to a vogue for round churches in imitation of the Holy Sepulchre, and Temple Church is one of just four such buildings still in use in England.

The round nave is the surviving part of the church of 1185. Its east arm was replaced in the 13th century by a longer aisled chancel. The aisles are as tall as the chancel proper, producing an east end of three equal gables, reminiscent of Cornish churches. The new aisled chancel

RIGHT *This distinguished Early English aisled chancel was consecrated in 1240 as a new east arm to the round nave.*

OPPOSITE *Heraclius, Patriarch of Jerusalem, consecrated this round church for the Knights Templar in 1185.*

was consecrated in 1240. The whole has been much restored. The west doorway is round-headed, with three main orders of shafts and much elaborate carving. All seems Norman, albeit late Norman. The porch, however, is rib-vaulted. This is the first instance to be noticed here of two different styles being used in the 12th-century work. The round itself is 18 metres (59 feet) in diameter and is divided into a nave and an ambulatory by a ring of six piers. The piers consist of four Purbeck marble shafts, two larger and two smaller, with shaft-rings. They have waterleaf capitals for the most part and support pointed arches. The ambulatory is rib-vaulted and has blank pointed arcading, but the windows are round-headed. The triforium has intersecting blind arches, a usual Norman feature. The chancel and its aisles are rib-vaulted and have triplets of lancets throughout, the middle lancet taller in each case.

The east end focuses on a pedimented reredos of 1682, which was carved by William Emmett. The stained glass in the east windows above, consisting of historical and heraldic subjects in roundels, is by

ABOVE LEFT The elaborately carved west doorway of the Norman round nave.

ABOVE RIGHT Effigies facing the font, on the south side of the round, include those of the family of William Marshall, Earl of Pembroke. Gilbert, fourth Earl, lies in the foreground.

RIGHT The Norman round nave is one of only four still in use in England, and it shelters several 13th-century Purbeck marble effigies of lay supporters of the Knights Templar.

Carl Edwards, 1957–8. Between the chancel and the nave there are the monuments to Edmund Plowden (died 1584), Treasurer of the Middle Temple, with a recumbent effigy under a coffered arch; and to Richard Martin (died 1618), Recorder of London, who kneels at a prayer-desk, also under an arch. To the west, there are the famous Purbeck effigies from the 13th century, representing lay supporters of the Templars. The one labelled as Robert de Ros is the best preserved. The rest, all heavily restored, include such prominent figures of history as Geoffrey de Mandeville and William Marshall, Earl of Pembroke.

Westminster Abbey

Collegiate Church of St Peter

Parliament Square

OPPOSITE Hawksmoor's familiar west towers, seen from Dean's Yard.

Westminster Abbey lies at the heart of English history. Monarchs of the nation for almost a millennium have come and gone through its doors and have been crowned and entombed within its walls. It owes its considerable importance to St Edward the Confessor, King of England from 1042 to 1066. He went to live at Westminster and decided to rebuild an existing Benedictine monastery of St Peter on a substantial scale, in accordance with the latest architectural ideas in Normandy, where he had been exiled for 25 years. He spent his later years in supervising the great project, and when he died, just days after the abbey's consecration, was buried in front of its high altar. For a king who was generally seen to have been weak, he came to have an extraordinary hold on his successors, as a symbol of legitimate royal authority, and in religious terms. He was acceptable both to the Normans, for William the Conqueror presented himself as Edward's legitimate successor, and to the English, for he was the last king of the ancient line of Wessex. Edward was canonized in 1161 and was enshrined two years later. In the 13th century, King Henry III rebuilt the whole church on Gothic lines – again in accordance with the latest architectural fashions in France – and erected a new and sumptuous shrine for St Edward, which was completed in 1269.

The most remarkable fact about the shrine is that it survives today with its relics intact. It is true that it was despoiled and dismantled at the Reformation, but St Edward's relics were not dishonoured and the shrine was restored (albeit clumsily) under Mary Tudor. The abbey has been the coronation church of the monarchs of England since William the Conqueror, and from even earlier in the 11th century it was a royal burial church. Some of the most famous monarchs in English history are entombed here in monuments that are among the foremost works of sculpture and architecture of their times. No church in London can even begin to compete with Westminster Abbey in the number and quality of its monuments.

Although the Confessor transformed the status of Westminster Abbey, he was not its founder. A Benedictine abbey had existed in the

10th century, and it seems probable that it went back further, to the reign of King Offa. But this 'prehistory' palls before the role of the Confessor. From his time, Westminster was a principal Benedictine abbey in England, until all the monasteries were dissolved under King Henry VIII. In 1560, under Queen Elizabeth I, the church was permanently redesignated as the Collegiate Church of St Peter, ruled by a Dean and Chapter and under the direct authority of the monarch as Visitor.

The abbey is built of Reigate stone, except for the east part – Henry VII's chapel – which is of Huddleston stone. It needs to be remembered, however, that what the visitor sees today is an outer skin that is the result of countless restorations. Restoration has been almost continuous under a succession of eminent architects. The appearance of two prominent parts of the exterior has been

greatly altered since the Middle Ages. The familiar west towers are largely the work of the 18th-century Baroque architect Nicholas Hawksmoor. The towers are notable for being so respectful of the design of the mediaeval nave. Secondly, the north transept front was substantially rebuilt by J. L. Pearson in the late 19th century, partly to his own designs. He was determined to be independent, an attitude shared by many eminent architects. (A 20th-century surveyor, Sir Walter Tapper, worked in alliance with an equally determined dean, William Foxley Norris, so that people spoke of decisions being taken by 'the Dean and Tapper'.)

The foundation stone of King Henry III's church was laid in 1245. By the time of the king's death in 1272, the east end had been completed, but only a part of the nave. The king's architect was Henry of Reyns, who referred to Reims Cathedral as a model. The interior of Westminster Abbey is markedly tall, on the French model; on the other hand, some of the details of its construction (such as the use of a ridge-rib in the east part) are English. It was not until the 14th century that the west part of the nave was built. Henry Yevele was the architect and remarkably he chose to follow the style of the earlier work, except in the west front, which he made Perpendicular. The interior therefore appears to date from one building campaign. The plan is cruciform, with aisled transepts, and a polygonal east end that allowed for five chapels to lead out of the ambulatory. The shrine was intended to be the focus, but the other determinant of the plan was the need to provide a large central space for coronations.

A screen was put up behind the high altar in 1440–1 by John Thirsk. He was also responsible for King Henry V's chantry chapel in 1437. It is possible that the former was needed to screen off activity in the latter. The back of the new screen was carved with scenes from the life of St Edward, as a mark of honour for his shrine. Nevertheless, the shrine ceased to be visible from the west. The final major structural change was the building of King Henry VII's chapel at the east end, in place of the Lady chapel, in 1503–12. Robert Janyns is most plausibly credited with the chapel's design, which is a four-

bay aisled work, with five radiating east chapels (as in Henry III's east end). The most striking feature is the exterior, in which secular elements stand out. The bay window and the turreted (and panelled) polygonal buttress are the chief features, but packed in a notably complicated pattern that leaves a continuously wavy outline. Since 1725, Henry VII's chapel has been the chapel of the Order of the Bath, whose banners add to its colour considerably.

The shrine of St Edward preserves most of its base, whose main purpose was to provide three niches on each side in which pilgrims could kneel. The base was dismantled in 1536 and when it was pieced together again 20 years later, various parts were placed upside-down or back to front. The Confessor's remains lie above. What has never been reinstated is the reliquary chest that surmounted the structure. Around the Confessor lie several mediaeval kings and their consorts. The first was King Henry III, whose monument is north of the shrine. The base was once inlaid with Cosmati mosaic work on both sides; the side to the aisle preserves it. His fine bronze effigy was made by William Torel in 1291, at the same time as he made the effigy of Eleanor of Castile (died 1290), the wife of King Edward I. Her tomb is surrounded by Thomas of Leighton's iron grille of 1294, which includes candle-holders. The final tomb on the north side is King Edward I's. It consists of a plain tomb-chest without an effigy. His grandson, King Edward III (died 1377), has an effigy of gilded bronze, probably by John Orchard, which rests on a base attributed to Henry Yevele. The six weepers on the aisle side are the king's children, including the Black Prince. The next monument is King Edward's consort, Philippa of Hainault, who has a black and white marble effigy by Jean de Liège. Finally, there is the monument to King Richard II and Anne of Bohemia. The broom plant (the *planta genista*, from which the name 'Plantagenet' was derived) and the chained hart appear as decorations on their clothing. In Henry VII's chapel, the effigies of its founder and his wife by Pietro Torrigiano are particularly fine works. The same sculptor was also responsible for the effigy of the King's mother, Margaret, Countess of Richmond, in the south aisle.

Until the end of the 16th century, monuments in the abbey were few. There were the great royal tombs, but relatively few others, and they were all of kinsmen of the monarchs, of royal officials or of members of the foundation. In the late Elizabethan and early Stuart decades, huge monuments started to appear. Lord Hunsdon (died 1596), Lord Chamberlain, was accorded one in St John the Baptist's chapel. King James erected in the early 1600s the monuments to his predecessor, Queen Elizabeth I (to the designs of Maximilian Colt) and to his mother, Mary, Queen of Scots (by Cornelius Cure), both with considerable architectural canopies; they stand in Henry VII's chapel. During the 17th century monuments without royal connections rapidly increased. From 1744, they were erected at parliamentary expense to war heroes. By that time, the abbey was crowded with monuments. Mention might be made here of Arnold Quellin's memorial to Thomas Thynne, which has a carving to show his murder in the Haymarket in 1682. The statue of Shakespeare in Poets' Corner (in the south transept) was carved by Peter Scheemakers in 1749 to William Kent's design. The two very prominent monuments that flank the entrance to the choir were carved by Michael Rysbrack to William Kent's designs. The one on the left (1731) is of Sir Isaac Newton, and the other (1733) is of the 1st Earl Stanhope. In the nave nearby, there are interesting brasses to 19th-century architects by their contemporaries. Sir George Gilbert Scott (died 1878) has a brass by G. E. Street, and Street himself (died 1881) was given one by G. F. Bodley. A recent brass is Earl Mountbatten's by Christopher Ironside (1985), near the west door. Two further memorials separated by 800 years merit a mention. The earlier one is that of Gilbert Crispin, Abbot, who died in 1117 or 1118, and consists of a worn figure with a crozier, in the south walk of the cloister. The other is that of the Unknown Warrior, who was buried at the west end in 1920: a commemoration of the First World War that was introduced in many countries.

In contrast to the monuments, there are fewer furnishings to discuss, but some are of the first importance. Near St Edward's shrine, there is the abbey's best-known ancient furnishing: the coronation chair of 1308, made of oak, with a tall gable at the back, and intended to house beneath it the Stone of Scone, which King Edward I had captured in Scotland. The pavements around the shrine and in the sanctuary are important Cosmati works commissioned by Abbot Ware in 1268. Sir George Gilbert Scott was responsible for the present high altar and the west face of the reredos. The choir-stalls, which occupy part of the crossing and part of the nave, are by Edward Blore, 1844–8. The great chandeliers of Waterford glass were donated in 1965.

The abbey church is a stupendous survival, but it needs to be remembered also that buildings from the mediaeval monastery survive to the south, including the whole cloister, minor parts of the Confessor's buildings and the chapter house, which Sir George Gilbert Scott restored. The buildings house, among other things, the important library and a worthy museum.

FAR LEFT The north transept is crowded with statues of statesmen. Gladstone's distinctive features stand out second from the right.

LEFT The tomb of King Henry III, who rebuilt the abbey in the 13th century, seen from the Confessor's chapel.

ABOVE Shakespeare's quizzical statue, designed by William Kent and carved by Scheemakers, stands out in Poets' Corner.

RIGHT The nave looking west from Edward the Confessor's Shrine, with Yevele's Perpendicular west window in the background. The great height of the interior is clearly shown in this view.

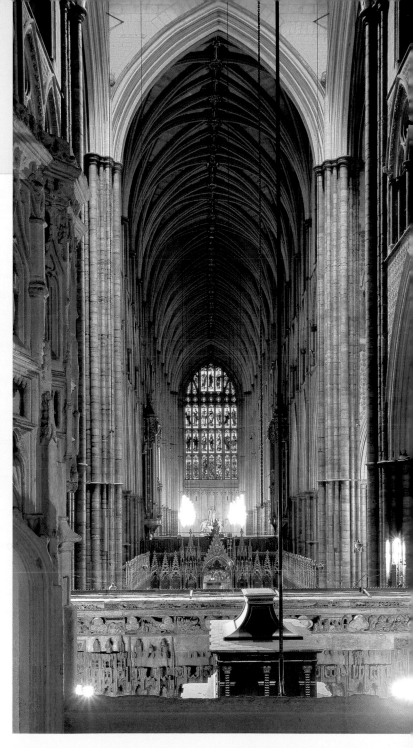

Westminster Cathedral

Francis Street

OPPOSITE *View of the high altar and its baldacchino, and the great hanging rood, both by J. F. Bentley.*

The campanile of Westminster Cathedral soars above the buildings and bustle of London's Victoria like an exclamation of astonishment. This principal Roman Catholic church in London is no less striking for its distinctive Byzantine style today than when it was completed in 1903. Richard Norman Shaw said of it: 'It is like a revelation after the feeble Gothic stuff on which we have been mainly fed for the last half-century.' It was the intention of its founder, Herbert, Cardinal Vaughan, that the long-intended cathedral should be built quickly and should soon be free from debt. The foundation stone was laid in 1895 and so the great structure took just eight years to build, which is perhaps the most remarkable fact of the scheme. (St Paul's Cathedral took 35 years to build, and Truro Cathedral, Westminster's contemporary, 30 years.) The debt was extinguished by 1910, when the cathedral was consecrated. It had cost £253,000. By then, Cardinal Vaughan had died – his funeral was the first great service in the building – and his successor had begun the long process of adorning its interior.

It is sometimes stated that as the first Archbishop of Westminster was appointed in 1850 and Westminster Cathedral was started only in 1895, the archbishops' policy towards building a cathedral had altered over that period. Cardinal Vaughan's wish to build is contrasted with his predecessor, Cardinal Manning's public identification with the poor and emphasis on building schools. In fact, Manning had made many preparations for building a cathedral, including the gradual assembly of a substantial site and the raising of much money. He even approved an ambitious Gothic design by Henry Clutton. He considered that Westminster needed a cathedral 'proportionate to the chief diocese of the Catholic Church in England, and to the chief city of the British Empire'. But the money to build was insufficient. As for Cardinal Vaughan, it is often forgotten that he founded the Mill Hill Fathers, a significant missionary order, and established the Catholic Social Union. His concern for the wider Church was obvious enough. What was striking about his decision to build a cathedral was his wish to impose

a tight grip on the scheme: he wanted the shell to be built quickly and relatively cheaply so that it could be adorned gradually while it was already in use. He particularly wanted a building in which the divine office could be recited and sung daily. To attain that aim, he had the strange idea of bringing Benedictine monks from Downside to Ealing, from where they would commute to Westminster. When this plan faltered, he had the even stranger idea of bringing French Benedictine monks from Solesmes (who were renowned for their Gregorian chant, or plainsong), which ruffled many feathers. In the end, his own diocesan clergy fulfilled the role.

John Francis Bentley (1839–1902) designed the cathedral, for which he drew inspiration from Santa Sophia in Constantinople, the most famous of all Byzantine churches, and from the ancient churches of Ravenna, where he admired the carved capitals and the early mosaics. He aimed at an early Christian style rather than a purely Byzantine one, and Ravenna was an ideal source, for there East had met West. Bentley had at his disposal at Westminster a rectangular site, at the east end of which he had to build a hall and substantial houses for the archbishop and his clergy. The west end fronted a road running parallel with Victoria Street, which was lined with tall commercial and residential buildings. The cathedral was hidden from Victoria Street until 1975. So Bentley set back the west front of the body of the church behind a narthex, which was given an entrance more Italianate than Byzantine. The great campanile, 86.6 metres (284 feet) high, was placed on the left. Much has

been made of the piazza created in 1975 between the west door and Victoria Street. The buildings that flank the piazza, however, are so unsympathetic to the cathedral that the scheme jars horribly. The cathedral belongs so much better with the contemporary mansion flats in Ambrosden Avenue and Morpeth Terrace, which share the cathedral's scheme of red brick with stone bands. The buildings that used to stand in Ashley Place fitted in well with this pattern.

The nave consists of three big domed bays, 18.3 metres (60 feet) wide, with narrow aisles, and outer chapels beyond them. All the buttressing of the nave is internal. The transepts open out of the third bay from the west, but they do not extend beyond the walls of the nave's chapels. The gallery runs across the transepts' arches. At the east end, a fourth domed bay serves as the sanctuary, which is flanked by very narrow aisles and then by apsidal chapels: the Blessed Sacrament chapel on the north and the Lady chapel on the south. The large apse behind the sanctuary houses the choir. The most conspicuous windows are semicircular and are of Byzantine inspiration. The nave is so wide and the transepts relatively shallow, that there is little sense of a crossing. The focus is firmly on the raised sanctuary and on the high altar under its Italianate baldacchino.

Bentley himself began the furnishing and adornment of the interior. He designed the great baldacchino in 1901, which was made by Farmer & Brindley, and the huge cross that hangs above the sanctuary. The octagonal font in the south-west corner also is Bentley's, inspired by Ravenna. He planned to clad the interior with coloured marbles and to decorate the vaults with mosaics, to make what he called a 'veneered building'. This work proceeded gradually, with close attention paid to what Bentley would have wanted, even so late as the 1960s. He personally worked on the Holy Souls' chapel next to the campanile; the mosaics there were by Christian Symons. The chapel of St Gregory and St Augustine, on the south side, was also decorated at an early date. Clayton & Bell executed the mosaics, which depict saints of the early English Church. (It was in this chapel that Cardinal Hume was buried in 1999.) In 1915 St

Andrew's chapel, also on the south side, was furnished at the expense of the 4th Marquess of Bute. His artist was R. W. S. Weir, who produced interesting ceiling mosaics of Patras, Constantinople, but more remarkable is Ernest Gimson's set of stalls, made of ebony inlaid with ivory. They represent work of a very high order. St Paul's chapel, to the east, has a floor of white Pentelic marble inlaid with red and green porphyry, which was made in the 1930s to the designs of Edward Hutton, the writer on Italian art. The Lady chapel has mosaics by G. W. Pownall, 1931–2. The Blessed Sacrament chapel, north of the sanctuary, was furnished by John Marshall early in the 20th century but was decorated in mosaic only in 1953–61, by Boris Anrep. Much money for this chapel was raised in Spain and South America by the founder's brother, Father Kenelm Vaughan.

The great pulpit, in early Christian style, was designed by C. A. Leonori in 1899. It was raised on columns in 1934. Just east of it there is a 15th-century alabaster statue of the Virgin and Child, known as Our Lady of Westminster. The large

panels of the Stations of the Cross were fitted in 1914–18 and were carved in low relief in Hoptonwood stone by Eric Gill. They show a marvellous sense of tense solemnity. The first Station, for example, gives a due sense of Roman grandeur in Pontius Pilate's throne, the arcading in the background and in the ceremony of washing his hands. The lettering is magnificent. These Stations stand out for their skill and yet they are reticent enough to fit in well with the architecture. In front of the sanctuary steps, an inscription recalls Pope John Paul II's Mass here in 1982, which was the first celebrated in England by a reigning Pope. The English Martyrs' chapel in the north aisle has the shrine of St. John Southworth, who was martyred at Tyburn in 1654. The Vaughan chantry further east has a monument of the founder, designed by John Marshall, with an effigy by J. Adams-Acton.

The musical tradition here is a very fine one. The first Master of Music (1901–24) was Sir Richard Terry, whose appointment by Vaughan was an astute and excellent choice. The cathedral's choir is one of the best in England.

All Saints
Margaret Street

ABOVE RIGHT The mural tiles were designed by Alexander Gibbs. This panel on the north wall depicts the adoration of the Shepherds and the Magi.

OPPOSITE The chancel is emphasized in this important Anglo-Catholic church, and is slightly taller than the nave.

London has a vast number of Victorian churches, which were among the major works of the leading architects of the time, but All Saints' has a unique place in the firmament, for it was built as a model church by those who had the greatest influence in High Church circles. Alexander Beresford-Hope, its principal benefactor, wanted to build not an ordinary parish church but a 'higher and more minster-like type'. He led the Ecclesiological Society, which campaigned for Gothic churches to be used for worship along Tractarian lines. The society was keen to put its ideas into practice and relished the chance to build a model church.

All Saints' was designed by William Butterfield and built in 1850–9. It has a markedly cramped site, a disadvantage for a model church in particular, but the architect placed his buildings to good effect. The domestic buildings were divided on either side of a small courtyard, with a gabled gateway in the middle. The church rises at the back. Three features attract the eye: a substantial porch; a tall pinnacle to the right of it; and the slim tower and spire, 70 metres (230 feet) high, to which the

pinnacle points. The church is built in red brick with bands of black brick and stone. Butterfield became known for his 'structural polychrome' and for his use of brick. One external feature that is instructive is that the chancel's roof is slightly higher than the nave's, for the Ecclesiologists preached incessantly on the importance of a substantial chancel.

The interior is tall and wide, but the nave is just three bays long. To this we must add the deep chancel and its chapels. The arcades are supported on red granite columns with black marble plinths. The south-west corner, under the tower, serves as a baptistery. A low marble wall divides the chancel from the nave, and low screens divide the chancel from its chapels. The lightly stained screen at the east end of the south aisle was designed by Laurence King in 1962; it makes less effort to fit in than anything else. Many artists have adorned the church. The paintings on the east wall are Sir Ninian Comper's from 1909. There are two tiers with seven panels each, plus one further panel at the top. Comper also carried out the paintings on the north and south sanctuary walls (in 1914), installed the hanging pyx (in 1930) and fitted out the Lady chapel, north of the chancel, in 1911. Alexander Gibbs designed the Tree of Jesse in the five-light west window (1877), and also the windows of the south aisle, and provided the mural tiles on the north wall (1873). Floor tiles were supplied by the firm of Minton. The prominent marble pulpit is Butterfield's.

The chancel features numerous panels painted by Sir Ninian Comper. He also installed the hanging pyx and fitted out the Lady chapel.

The west window, made in 1877 by Alexander Gibbs, depicts the Tree of Jesse.

The highly coloured marble pulpit was one of Butterfield's original furnishings.

Farm Street Church

Church of the Immaculate Conception

Mount Street

OPPOSITE The interior looking east, which has been thoroughly restored in recent years, focuses on Pugin's high altar and on Hardman's east window.

This is the principal London church of the Jesuits, St Ignatius Loyola's 'shock troops' of the Counter-Reformation, who preside here over a fine work of the Victorian Gothic Revival. It is arguably the finest Catholic church of that style in London, which is all the more creditable as the nave was built early in the Gothic Revival in 1844–9 and no fewer than three architects had a major part in designing the whole. The specific style is 14th-century Decorated, but represented here in an exuberant, 'flowing' manner. Much of the ornate effect of the interior comes from the numerous side chapels with their altarpieces and statues. In recent years much restoration has been undertaken to produce a mediaeval effect of painted surfaces and statues, and stained glass and sculpture. The roof has been excellently repainted, the benches have been re-varnished and, more remarkably, the roundels between the arches have been filled for the first time (in 1996) with mosaics, by Filomena Monteiro, which provide the full text of the *Ave Maria* in Latin, with accompanying symbols.

J. J. Scoles designed the aisled nave and chancel. They are tall, eight bays long, and end in a fine nine-light east window, which was inspired by Carlisle Cathedral. There is a chancel arch, but as it is tall and shelters no rood screen, the interior is practically undivided. The high altar was designed by A. W. N. Pugin, the great master of the Gothic Revival. It was made of Caen stone, with much gilding. The reredos consists of crocketed pinnacles over gabled statue niches, with larger (and projecting) flanking niches and a still larger one in the centre to house the tabernacle. Above the altarpiece there are two mosaic panels, one of the Annunciation and one of the Coronation of the Virgin, made in 1875. The east window is filled with stained glass representing the Tree of Jesse, made by John Hardman & Company, 1912. The window was once lower than it is today; it was raised to stand clear of the altar and of the mosaic panels. The sanctuary was also raised to good effect to make the east end the clear focus of the interior. It was further embellished with panelling of dark green Genoese marble and Nottinghamshire alabaster. The marble

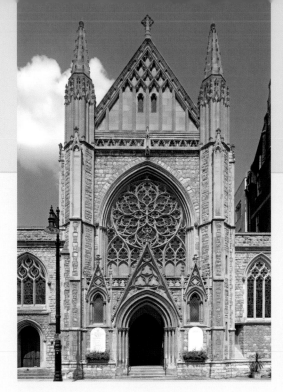

sanctuary rail dates from 1901. At its south side (to the right) there is a wooden statue of the Virgin Mary, given in 1868 and placed under a tall canopy.

To the right of the high altar there is the Sacred Heart chapel, which Henry Clutton added in 1858–9. The front of the altar has a brass relief of St Joseph by Pfeiffer and above the altar there is a mural painting by Molitor. Notice the two angels that flank the tabernacle: they were the work of J. F. Bentley when he was a clerk in Clutton's office. He went on to design Westminster Cathedral. Clutton himself added the outer south aisle in 1878, consisting of three chapels, whose altars were designed by A. E. Purdie. More flamboyant is the outer north aisle, by W. H. Romaine Walker, 1898–1903. The chapels on that side are placed at right angles to the nave, except for the octagonal Calvary chapel at the west end and the chapel of St Ignatius at the east. The Calvary chapel became a baptistery in 1966, when the church became a parish church for the first

time. St Ignatius Loyola was the founder of the Jesuits and has a larger chapel, outside which an impressive black-clad statue is placed: black because of the Jesuits' habit or dress, which is rendered here in Polyphant marble. At the west end of the church, St Anthony of Padua's statue is equally striking in white Carrara marble. The (internal) buttresses for the nave in this aisle skilfully shelter the confessionals. In early days, confession was offered in various languages, reflecting, as Henry James said of St Maria Maggiore in Rome, 'the polyglot sinfulness of the world'.

Although the church is named after the Immaculate Conception, it is widely known as Farm Street Church. Its west façade on that street, modelled on Beauvais Cathedral, is the one part of the exterior that can be seen to good effect. A rose is placed above the main west window, which has stained glass of 1953 by Evie Hone, depicting the Passion.

FAR LEFT The west front in Farm Street, which incorporates a rose window, was modelled on Beauvais Cathedral.

LEFT In 1996 the roundels between the arches of the nave were decorated for the first time: the central panels make up the text of the Ave Maria.

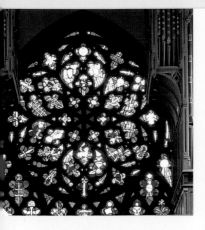

ABOVE The rose window at the west end is filled with stained glass of the Passion, by Evie Hone, 1953.

RIGHT The great proponent of the Victorian Gothic Revival, A. W. N. Pugin, designed this high altar. His mastery of Gothic detail surpassed that of his contemporaries.

St Augustine
Kilburn Park Road

HISTORY
- Built in 1871–80 by J. L. Pearson for Richard Carr Kirkpatrick, Anglo-Catholic priest
- The tower and spire were added in 1897–8
- Embellished by Sir Giles Gilbert Scott in the 20th century
- One of London's most important Victorian churches

OF SPECIAL INTEREST
- The north-west tower and spire, rising to 77.4 metres (254 feet)
- The vaulting throughout the church
- The stone chancel screen
- The substantial collection of Victorian stained glass

It is a common feature in the history of the Free Churches that a new church was often formed by a split in an existing one, and that such a split frequently centred on the choice of a new pastor. St Augustine's is a rare instance of this process in the Church of England, for its founder, Richard Carr Kirkpatrick, felt compelled to found a new Anglo-Catholic parish in Kilburn when his existing ministry at St Mary's, Priory Road, was upset by a new Evangelical incumbent. He presided over the erection of an extraordinary church, which is one of the most important Victorian buildings in London.

OPPOSITE AND RIGHT The high altar and the stone screen which separate it from the nave have lavish sculptured adornment. Victorian architects usually worked with their own groups of craftsmen to fit out and decorate their churches.

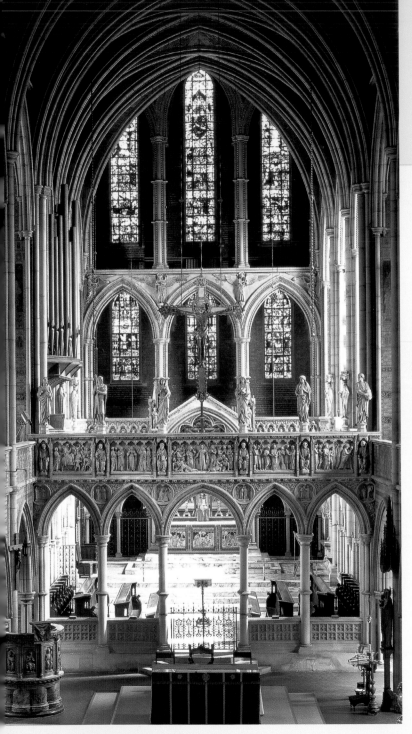

St Augustine's parish began in 1870 in the usual 'iron church', but plans were soon made for a permanent replacement by J. L. Pearson. The foundation stone was laid in 1871 and the church was consecrated in 1880. Not until 1897–8 were the tower and spire constructed at the north-west corner. Many Victorian churches were always to lack ambitious spires, and so it is a matter for thanksgiving that one was added to complete this exceptional design. The spire is 77.4 metres (254 feet) high.

The church is built in red brick in Pearson's usual 13th-century style. As you approach its doorway under the tower, that badge of the 13th century – dog-tooth moulding – is at once apparent. All the windows except one are tall lancets. The exception is the huge rose window in the west gable. There are angle turrets at the east and west ends, and a sizeable flèche at the crossing. The interior is an impressive sight, for it is vaulted throughout and has a gallery that runs round the church, even across the openings into the transepts. A vaulted interior was Pearson's trademark. There are double aisles because of internal buttressing. East of the north transept lies the Lady chapel, and on the south there is the apsidal St Michael's chapel. There is a stone screen of five arches to mark the division between nave and chancel.

In the 20th century, Sir Giles Gilbert Scott enhanced Pearson's reredos for the high altar; he also designed the Lady chapel's reredos and the Stations of the Cross. The firm of Clayton & Bell executed the mural paintings and made the numerous stained-glass windows. If ever a Victorian church lived up to the mediaeval ideal of a pictorial exposition of Scripture and the Christian faith, it was St Augustine's. Practically every major Biblical story is represented, and there are also many windows depicting later saints. St Augustine himself features in the lower tier of east windows, and the nave aisle windows represent saints of the early English Church. The rose window tells the story of Creation.

St Clement Danes

Strand

OPPOSITE ABOVE An aisle view shows the glass-fronted cases that contain RAF rolls of honour.

OPPOSITE BELOW St Clement's became the central church of the RAF after a distinguished restoration in 1955–8. The unusually wide central aisle shows some of the hundreds of RAF squadron badges in slate set into the floor.

St Clement Danes has served as the central church of the Royal Air Force since 1958, following a distinguished restoration by Anthony Lloyd in 1955–8 to repair the ravages of bombing in 1941. The body of the church had been rebuilt by Sir Christopher Wren in 1680–2, but the tower had been the work of Joshua Marshall in 1669–70, and to that tower James Gibbs had added the familiar steeple in 1719–20.

The church has the advantage of a spacious island site, where Aldwych and the Strand meet. Statues of Lord Dowding, the victor of the Battle of Britain, and Sir Arthur 'Bomber' Harris introduce the RAF connection. The tall west tower and steeple present a curious mixture of styles. The doorway is an early Classical work. Then there are two Y-traceried windows above, separated by a Wren-style porthole. Finally, above the clock-faces, there are belfry windows with 'Gibbs surrounds' and a steeple of three receding, open-arched octagonal stages, the middle one with a concave architrave, and all liberally adorned with urns.

The spacious, galleried interior immediately presents to the eye a mass of darkly stained woodwork, which is notably more faithful to a Wren interior than the light-coloured woodwork introduced into many restorations of Wren's churches. Square, panelled piers support the galleries, above which Corinthian columns rise to carry block entablatures, coffered arches and the tunnel-vault of the nave. The galleries are groin-vaulted. The east end consists of a quadrant bay on each side and an apse. The capitals are gilded, as are the cherubim and the surrounds of heraldic shields above the arcades. Dominating all these features are the Stuart royal arms, placed over the east arch.

The Wren-style reredos has two large arched panels painted by Ruskin Spear to represent the Annunciation. The east window depicts Christ in glory, by Carl Edwards. Also by him are the Virgin and Child to the north, and the pietà to the south. On each side of the sanctuary there is a canopied bishop's chair. The pulpit is the highly carved 17th-century original, but the lectern is a remarkably ornate work of postwar date, by Anthony Lloyd. The west gallery houses the organ by Ralph Downes,

which has a distinguished case featuring four towers surmounted by urns and embellished with much gilding. Over 700 RAF squadron badges in slate are set into the floor, with a larger one for the whole RAF at the west end, and this principal badge is surrounded by overseas allies' badges. Below the aisle windows there are glass-fronted cases that contain RAF rolls of honour. Carved stalls are provided at the west end for the commanders of the RAF.

St Cyprian's
Glentworth Street

RIGHT The rood, with figures of the Virgin Mary and St John and two flanking angels, is a fine example of a type of furnishing revived in the Church of England in the early 20th century.

OPPOSITE Comper's late mediaeval interior in the East Anglian style focuses on the great rood screen stretching across the church, and on the high altar and the east window beyond.

St Cyprian's owes its existence to a distinguished priest, Charles Gutch, who nevertheless died before it was built. He was an Anglo-Catholic pioneer, who settled in St Marylebone in 1866. He ran a highly successful parish for 30 years – a hero of the Victorian Church – and he ought to have been able to build a permanent church. Instead, he had to make do with two converted houses, because the local landowner, Viscount Portman, disliked Gutch's High Churchmanship and declined to make a site available. After Gutch died, a site was reluctantly offered and so in 1902–3 a church was duly built. Ninian Comper was chosen to design it, and he produced an important Anglo-Catholic church in an East Anglian Perpendicular style, which he proceeded to fit out and adorn over several decades.

Why St Cyprian's? The saint was a 3rd-century Bishop of Carthage, whose letters struck Charles Gutch as providing a model for his own

ministry. The Bishop of London preferred an Apostle, but it was pointed out that many recent churches had been named after saints other than Apostles. Gutch won the day and his parish kept its distinctive name.

The church is a plain towerless rectangle in red brick. It has seven-bay arcades without structural division. All the details are Perpendicular. The main east window has five transomed lights and the chancel chapels have four-light windows. The north aisle windows have simpler tracery than those on the south, which face Glentworth Street. The church concentrates its riches at the east end. A painted and gilded rood screen, which was completed in 1924, is the most striking fitting. It starts two bays from the east end and stretches across nave and aisles. There are 32 painted figures in its lower panels and a loft with elaborate coving. Above, there is a rood, with the Virgin Mary and St John, and two angels at the sides, all gilded. The tall font cover is also inspired by 15th-century East Anglian examples, but it does incorporate some Classical elements, too, for Comper increasingly mixed his styles; it is the one ornate fitting at the west end. This part of the church was not completed until 1930. The high altar is one of Comper's 'English altars', surrounded by curtains, a dossal, and angels on top of riddel posts. A canopy of honour that he painted as late as 1948 hangs high above it. The altar has been splendidly restored quite recently. The stained glass shows Comper's usual predominant blues and yellows. St Cyprian appears in the main east window. The oak pulpit, with linenfold panels and a tester, is in a later, Elizabethan, style.

St George's

St George Street, south of Hanover Square

HISTORY

- Built in 1721–5 by John James
- One of the Fifty New Churches
- George Frederick Handel was a parishioner and tested candidates for the office of organist here
- Theodore Roosevelt, President of the USA, was married here
- H. H. Asquith, George Eliot, Marconi, Grimaldi the clown and Disraeli were all married here

OF SPECIAL INTEREST

- The west portico, with the pair of dogs and the obelisks
- The east window, which contains 16th-century Flemish glass
- The names of past churchwardens on the gallery fronts
- The organ in the west gallery

RIGHT The interior, seen from gallery level, preserves its Georgian ensemble but incorporates such later alterations as the black and white marble flooring.

OPPOSITE The organ in the west gallery was first built in 1725 by Gerard Smith, with Handel's advice. It was last rebuilt by Harrison & Harrison in 1972.

The dedication of this fashionable London church and the name of the nearby square are trumpetings of King George I, the first monarch of the House of Hanover. A great ornament of his court, George Frederick Handel, the famous composer, was a parishioner here from 1724 to 1759. Handel's house still stands in Brook Street (next door, incongruously, to that of Jimi Hendrix). Handel was in very grand company, for the first Vestry (or parochial council) of St George's in 1725 included no fewer than seven dukes and fourteen earls. Some of their names appear on the gallery fronts to mark their service as churchwardens.

St George's was built in 1721–5 to the designs of John James as one of the Fifty New Churches. James is generally regarded as a competent but less original architect than his contemporaries, such as Hawksmoor and Gibbs, and this church is sometimes given faint praise as a result.

strength to a wall that might have been dull. The east elevation features a substantial Venetian window. The unexpected statues of dogs under the portico (two seated pointers) were brought from a shop in Conduit Street that was bombed in 1940. The obelisks were lamp standards.

The interior has galleries that are supported on square piers and that carry in turn four-bay arcades on Corinthian columns with gilded capitals. There is a straight entablature and a segmental ceiling. The east end is slightly recessed behind a wide, segmental arch. Sir Arthur Blomfield arranged the choir and laid down the black and white marble floor. His nephew, Reginald Blomfield, introduced the screens north and south of the choir in 1926. The reredos is a wide one, with canted ends, and chiefly features a rather dark painting of the Last Supper by William Kent. The stained glass in the east window and in the gallery east windows has a distinguished history. It is Flemish glass that was made in about 1525 for a Carmelite church in Antwerp by Arnold of Nijmegen; it was later placed in a church at Malines. Thomas Willement adapted it for St George's in 1840. The glass depicts the Tree of Jesse and was given by the Holy Roman Emperor, Charles V, in thanksgiving for the return of a ship, the *Victoria*, from Magellan's circumnavigation. Willement replaced the image of the Emperor above the figure of Jesse with that of St George. In the original window, God the Father appeared at the top, but the figure was not used here and was taken instead to Wilton Parish Church near Salisbury. The pulpit is original, but its tester was removed in 1871 and it was

This is perhaps a little unfair, as the Commissioners of the 1711 Act had ordered James to keep the cost to £10,000. Given that this sum was only a quarter of the total spent on St John's, Smith Square, James could not be expansive. Nevertheless, his treatment of that perennial problem of 18th-century church design, the west end, is successful here. He deployed a hexastyle Corinthian portico – one of the first three for a London church – to stand forward in St George Street by straddling the pavement, for the west elevation was the only one that was afforded any prominence by the church's site. He combined the portico with a modest but appropriate tower, which avoids the impression of riding on the roof, as at St Martin-in-the-Fields; and yet it was the example of St Martin's that was copied elsewhere. The tower here is similar to Wren's cupola for the Royal Hospital at Chelsea and also to some of the later steeples of his City churches. The north elevation, however, which faces Maddox Street, evidently took Hawksmoor's ideas as models, and brought an impression of

BELOW LEFT One of the east windows, whose glass was originally made for a Carmelite church in Antwerp in 1525 by gift of the Holy Roman Emperor Charles V.

BELOW RIGHT The gallery fronts are inscribed with the names of past churchwardens. The first Vestry, or parochial council, of 1725, included seven dukes and fourteen earls.

lowered in 1894. It stands on six fluted Corinthian columns and boasts fine wrought-iron stairs.

The west gallery houses an organ that was first built by Gerard Smith in 1725. It was last rebuilt by Harrison & Harrison in 1972, and it is housed in a splendid five-towered case. Handel was naturally asked about the suitability of the organ, and devised tests for those who applied to be organist. Imagine being tested by Handel!

St George's has been noted for its fashionable weddings since Georgian times. Among those married here were the Duke of Sussex (the sixth son of King George III); Disraeli; the future American President, Theodore Roosevelt, who was described as a 'ranchman'; Joseph Grimaldi the clown; H. H. Asquith, later Prime Minister, whose wedding was attended by three other politicians who served in that office; George Eliot; and Marconi.

St Margaret's Church
St Margaret Street

HISTORY
- The present building was consecrated in 1523
- Built by Robert Stowell, master mason of Westminster Abbey, and by Thomas and Henry Redman
- Probably founded in the 11th or 12th century
- 'Parish church' of the House of Commons
- Burial place of William Caxton, 1491
- Burial place of Sir Walter Raleigh after his execution
- Sir Winston Churchill was married here in 1908

OF SPECIAL INTEREST
- 16th-century Flemish glass in the east window
- Central panel of the reredos by Siffron Alken, 1758
- Monument to Cornelius Vandun in the north aisle
- West window of the north aisle, depicting John Milton
- Bust of King Charles I outside the east end

The 'parish church' of the House of Commons, St Margaret's stands between Westminster Abbey and the Houses of Parliament, and owes its prominence to both. For centuries it has been run in tandem with the abbey; indeed, it was founded to serve the layfolk who lived around the great monastery. As for its other great neighbour, St Margaret's became the church of the House of Commons in 1614, and ever since there have been parliamentary services within its walls. The 17th-century Puritans disliked the abbey's ceremonial, and thought St Margaret's would be more palatable. Cromwell himself worshipped here, but after Hamo Thornycroft's statue of him appeared across the road outside Westminster Hall in 1899, a riposte was eventually arranged in the form of a lead bust of King Charles I in a niche at the church's east end.

RIGHT The interior is a late mediaeval example which is undivided from west to east. It was much rearranged by Sir George Gilbert Scott in 1877.

BELOW *The east window has 16th-century stained glass which was made to commemorate either King Henry VIII's marriage to Catherine of Aragon, or the earlier betrothal to her of his elder brother, Arthur.*

The building we see today was consecrated in 1523. Robert Stowell, the abbey's master mason, was its first architect, and he was followed by Thomas and Henry Redman. John Islip, the last great Abbot of Westminster, paid for the chancel. John James partly rebuilt the north-west tower in 1734–8 and encased the church in Portland stone. J. L. Pearson added the stately west and south-east porches.

Inside, the arcades and the clerestory windows form an unbroken procession to the east end. Sir George Gilbert Scott's restoration of 1877 was largely responsible for the appearance of the interior, for he replaced most of the furnishings. The east end, however, has much earlier elements. The stained glass in the prominent east window was made either for King Henry VIII and Catherine of Aragon, or for his brother, Arthur, who had previously been due to marry her. It is pictorial, Renaissance glass – forming a picture across the lights – and has a marked blue background. The reredos, a triptych, has a central panel carved in limewood by Siffron Alken, 1758, of the Supper at Emmaus. The north aisle's west window, by Clayton & Bell, is a memorial to John Milton, the blind poet who was a parishioner here. He is shown in the second light from the left, dictating *Paradise Lost* to his daughter.

A popular monument is a frontal bust in the north aisle to Cornelius Vandun (died 1577), a Yeoman of the Guard. Another commemorates Wenceslaus Hollar (died 1677), who drew the famous panorama of London c. 1636–42. In the south aisle is a recumbent effigy of Mary, Lady Dudley (died 1600), sister of Lord Howard of Effingham, the commander against the Spanish Armada. Among those buried here are William Caxton, the first English printer (died 1491); Sir Walter Raleigh (died 1618), the explorer and commander, who was executed nearby in Old Palace Yard; and Admiral Blake (died 1657), Cromwell's admiral.

St Martin-in-the-Fields
Trafalgar Square

OPPOSITE *The prominent west front includes the royal arms in the tympanum of the portico.*

Trafalgar Square is so central and important a public space in central London that the church of St Martin-in-the-Fields at its north-east corner seems to have the most prominent site of any church in the city. Since Dick Sheppard's time as Vicar (1914–27), it has also had a national and international role, through its broadcasting, publications and music. Before the square was laid out in the 1820s, however, the church was relatively hidden away in St Martin's Lane, north of the main road that went from the Strand to Whitehall. St Martin's parish was apparently taken out of St Margaret's parish when almost everywhere west of the City of London was under the sway of Westminster Abbey. Yet modern archaeology has shown that St Martin's stands in the middle of the site of Lundenwic, the London of the 8th and 9th centuries, about which St Bede the Venerable wrote. Lundenwic obviously had its churches; was there one where St Martin's now stands? It so happens that St Martin lent his name to a disproportionate number of early English churches. It would be fitting if such a prominent church did have an exceptionally early origin.

The present church was built in 1721–6 and was designed by James Gibbs. The architect's portrait may be seen on the staircase in the north-west corner, and there was once a bust of him by Rysbrack, but that is now in the Victoria and Albert Museum. The church's most familiar element is its grand Corinthian portico, whose six columns are raised on a flight of steps above St Martin's Lane. The portico's tympanum bears the arms of King George I, who was not only the reigning monarch when the church was new, but was also its churchwarden. St Martin's is the parish church of St James's Palace and Buckingham Palace, and its registers have many royal entries. The Latin inscription on the entablature states that the parishioners of St Martin's built this sacred house of God in AD 1726.

The west tower stands behind the portico, but appears to sit on its roof. It actually surmounts a vestibule and is flanked by the staircases to the galleries. The combination of steeple and portico has been a model for many later churches in England and North America. The body of the

LEFT The east end, very light after the church's recent restoration, now focuses on the unusual new glazing of the east window.

RIGHT The columns of the nave support block entablatures and a vault that is adorned with gilded and painted plasterwork.

BELOW A view at gallery level, which was always an important part of an 18th-century church interior.

church has the usual two tiers of windows for a Georgian galleried church, but here the windows each have a 'Gibbs surround', in which raised blocks of stone are spaced up the sides and round the arch. It was a widespread motif in the 18th century. Between the windows there are giant Corinthian pilasters and, in the east and west bays, giant recessed columns, which give a sense of monumentality. A row of urns was intended to surmount the balustrade above, but no urns were ever made. The east end has a large Venetian window. The church is fortunate in its surroundings. It has a block of land to itself, enclosed by robust original railings: a Classical temple on a temple mount. On its north side it faces the former vestry hall and former parochial school, and to the east there are the buildings of Nash's West Strand Improvements, all sympathetic Georgian neighbours.

There is a wide, spacious nave, for the galleries are set well back and the tall columns support block entablatures, from which rise a shallow tunnel-vault. There is no clerestory. The ceiling is divided into gilded and painted plasterwork panels by Artari and Bagutti, and the royal arms are prominently placed over the chancel arch. The north-east and south-east corners have special pews at gallery level, with canted sides facing the nave. The one to the left is a royal pew, and that on the right an Admiralty pew, formerly bedecked with an array of naval flags. The body of the church has pews of 1799 which were later cut down, a fine pulpit of the same date, and a font of 1689, which came from the previous church. A portrait of Dick Sheppard hangs on the west wall,

and a chapel named after him is in the crypt on the south side. The church's modern reputation for an expansive ministry almost entirely derives from him.

Nell Gwyn was buried here when the previous church still stood. Also buried at St Martin's were Thomas Chippendale, the well-known craftsman, and Sir Winston Churchill (died 1688), the father of the 1st Duke of Marlborough and ancestor of the 20th-century statesman.

St Paul's Church

Bedford Street

One of the great first encounters in 20th-century theatre is that between Professor Henry Higgins and the flower-girl Eliza Doolittle in Shaw's *Pygmalion*. It takes place beneath the portico of St Paul's, Covent Garden, an apt theatrical setting for a church close to so many theatres. St Paul's has become known as the actors' church and has a large number of theatrical memorials.

St Paul's is all that is left of a remarkable 17th-century development. Francis Russell, the 4th Earl of Bedford, planned to build on his land in Covent Garden to replenish his family's finances. He secured a royal licence for the project, which stipulated that it must provide a 'distinguished ornament' to London; and he also secured the services of Inigo Jones, the most celebrated architect of the day. Jones designed a stately Classical square, which he called a piazza because of its Italian inspiration. On its west side, St Paul's was to stand. According to a well-known story, first recorded by Horace Walpole, the 18th-century gossip, Jones was warned by the Earl of Bedford to keep the expenses low. 'Well, then', Jones replied, 'you shall have the handsomest barn in England'.

RIGHT   The east portico in Covent Garden, where Professor Higgins met Eliza Doolittle in Pygmalion.

OPPOSITE LEFT   Modern memorials to Rattigan, Coward and Chaplin (right) from among many in 'the actors' church'.

OPPOSITE RIGHT   The interior, seen here facing east, was much reordered by William Butterfield in the 1870s.

St Paul's was built in 1631–3 but was not consecrated until 1638. In 1795 it was burnt, but was restored on the old lines by Thomas Hardwick. The building is a towerless oblong, with tall, arched windows, a notably overhanging roof and a prominent Tuscan portico to the piazza. The angle pillars are square, and the two between are round. The east end was intended to include the main entrance, and the altar was to be at the west end, but Archbishop Laud disallowed this arrangement, and it was reversed.

The interior is undivided, save for a Doric west gallery and a screen beneath. At one time the church had north and south galleries, but they were removed by William Butterfield in 1872. He also raised the east end, a typical Victorian move to make the altar more prominent. Fixed to the organ gallery are the royal arms and also the arms of the Dukes of Bedford, the historic patrons. The stained glass in the east windows is by Brian Thomas, 1968–9.

The church has many associations with famous Londoners. J. M. W. Turner and W. S. Gilbert were baptized here; and among those buried here have been Sir Peter Lely, the painter; Samuel Butler, the author of *Hudibras*; Grinling Gibbons, the celebrated carver; and Thomas Arne, who composed *Rule, Britannia!* Arne has a memorial on the north wall.

Covent Garden takes its name from the Abbot and *Convent* of Westminster, for Westminster Abbey once owned the land. The Reformation brought the property into the 1st Earl of Bedford's hands in 1552.

Westminster, St John's
Smith Square

HISTORY
- Built in 1713–28 by Thomas Archer
- One of the Fifty New Churches
- Bombed in 1941
- Restored by Marshall Sisson in 1965–9 for use as a concert hall

OF SPECIAL INTEREST
- The monumental north and south entrance fronts
- The organ by Johannes Klais, 1993, in a case of 1734
- The display of historical photographs in the crypt

Although Queen Anne likened it to a footstool and Dickens lampooned it as 'some petrified monster, frightful and gigantic, on its back with its legs in the air', St John's is nevertheless one of London's most important Baroque buildings. It was built in 1713–28 under the Fifty New Churches Act to the designs of Thomas Archer. St John's was bombed in 1941 and was restored by Marshall Sisson only in 1965–9, for use as a concert hall.

The church dominates Smith Square. The plan seems from the outside to be a Greek cross with quadrants filling the greater part of the angles. The north and south fronts were given the monumental treatment of huge Tuscan columns standing at the top of flights of steps, rising to broken pediments, and flanked by tall, circular towers with columns attached diagonally. The east and west ends have the one major motif of a substantial Venetian window.

Inside, despite Archer's attempts to create a tension between longitudinal and centralizing effects, the longitudinal is undoubtedly dominant. The one important furnishing is the organ, which was built in 1993 by Johannes Klais. It has a genuine English case of 1734, which accords well with the church.

ABOVE The monumental façades and corner towers of St John's dominate the modest square.

RIGHT The interior, facing the organ of 1993; this was the altar end before the war.

Westminster Methodist Central Hall

Storey's Gate

HISTORY

- Built in 1905–12 by Lanchester and Rickards
- Built by the Wesleyan Methodist Twentieth Century Fund, which commemorated the centenary of John Wesley's death in 1891
- Housed the first meeting of the United Nations General Assembly in 1946

OF SPECIAL INTEREST

- Plaque on the Tothill Street façade to mark the first meeting of the United Nations General Assembly
- Statue of John Wesley on the main landing
- The main hall

ABOVE The principal façade of Westminster Central Hall opposite Westminster Abbey.

ABOVE RIGHT The main hall is used for regular Methodist worship and for many secular meetings.

It might seem strange that a building of secular appearance that housed the first meeting of the United Nations General Assembly in 1946, should be one of Methodism's chief centres. It was opened in 1912 as the eventual result of a wish in 1891 to mark the centenary of John Wesley's death. In 1898 the Wesleyan Methodist Twentieth Century Fund was set up; it was popularly known as the 'Million Guinea Fund' because a million Methodists were encouraged to give a guinea each. Messrs Lanchester & Rickards won the competition to design the new building, and it was built in 1905–12.

The Central Hall is a huge Classical building, which occupies an entire block of land. It is close to Westminster Abbey but its style is in complete contrast to the mediaeval Gothic across the street. Neither does it compete in plan, for it is roughly square, with a considerable domed bulk. It certainly does not announce itself as a church. In fact, it houses numerous offices as well as the hall itself. A statue of John Wesley greets the visitor and an opulent grand staircase leads to a landing. The main hall lies behind. Over the years, it has been used for countless non-religious meetings, but it does of course play a continuous and leading role in English Methodism as its founders intended.

St Etheldreda's

Ely Place

HISTORY

- Surviving mediaeval chapel of the former London mansion of the Bishops of Ely
- Bought by the Institute of Charity (the Rosminians), a Roman Catholic order, in 1874
- Dates from *c.*1290, a good example of an early Decorated church
- Named after the foundress of the monastery at Ely in the 7th century
- Ely Place is referred to in Shakespeare's *Richard III*

OF SPECIAL INTEREST

- The east window by Joseph E. Nuttgens, 1952
- Statues of 16th- and 17th-century martyrs by Mary Blakeman, 1962–4
- Gabled reliquary at the east end, containing a relic of St Etheldreda
- West window by Charles Blakeman, 1964, commemorates martyrs from the London Charterhouse
- The screen at the west end by J. F. Bentley, 1897
- The crypt

ABOVE The west window depicts Carthusian monks who were martyred under King Henry VIII.

RIGHT The much-restored fabric of the nave dates from about 1290.

FAR RIGHT The stained glass in the east window was made by Joseph E. Nuttgens in 1952 and provides an excellent visual focus for the interior.

St Etheldreda's was originally the chapel in a palace of the Bishops of Ely, and recalls the pre-Reformation days when most mediaeval bishops, abbots and priors kept large houses in London; Lambeth Palace is the great survivor of such houses today. The Holborn church was owned by the Bishops of Ely until 1772, when the present Ely Place was built. In 1874 the church was bought by the Institute of Charity or Rosminians, a Roman Catholic order that had been founded in 1838 by Antonio Rosmini Serbati. This is therefore a rare case of a modern Catholic congregation occupying a mediaeval church, albeit a much restored one. A recent rector, Father Kit Cunningham, MBE, ran a 'Strawberrie Fair' in Ely Place for many years in aid of charity, in allusion to the strawberries grown at the mediaeval palace, mentioned in Shakespeare's *Richard III*.

St Etheldreda's is a typical two-storey mediaeval private chapel, of which St Stephen's in the Palace of Westminster was once the most prominent example in London, but whose crypt is the only part to survive. A close existing parallel to St Etheldreda's is the chapel of Prior Crauden at Ely itself, for they are of comparable date as well as type. Only the east end of St Etheldreda's can be seen from Ely Place. The entrance leads the visitor into a corridor on the south side and up a substantial flight of steps into the aisleless, rectangular upper church. The interior is dominated by the huge, five-light east window, which almost fills the wall. It has intersecting tracery that does not reach the apex but is crowned instead by a large sexfoil. Geometrical shapes enrich the heads of the lights. The design of this window mixes styles typical of the 13th and early 14th centuries; it is Decorated but not curvilinear. In 1952 the window was filled with stained glass by Joseph E. Nuttgens, a design that is in agreeable contrast to its jagged and stark postwar contemporaries elsewhere. God the Father is at the head of the window, and below in the tracery lights there are the Nine Orders of Angels, the ancient *chi-rho* symbol (the first two letters of 'Christ' in Greek), a symbol of the Holy Trinity, and the Greek letters *alpha* and *omega*, with which Christ referred to Himself as the beginning and the end. The middle light shows Christ the

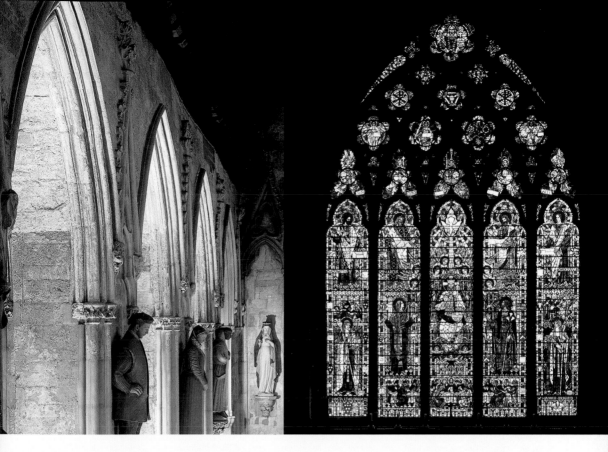

King surrounded by angels, with the dove of the Holy Spirit above. Christ is flanked by the Virgin Mary and St Joseph, and in the outer left-hand light by St Etheldreda, the church's patroness, who founded the monastery at Ely in 673. The Ely arms of three gold crowns on a red background can be seen. Above the principal figures are the four Evangelists holding the opening texts of their Gospels in Latin, and accompanied by their symbols: a man for Matthew, a lion for Mark, an ox for Luke and an eagle for John.

The west end has a screen of 1897 by J. F. Bentley, which divides off the first bay and supports the Lewis organ, also of 1897. The west window has stained glass of 1964 by Charles Blakeman, which depicts monks of the nearby London Charterhouse who were martyred in 1535 for denying King Henry VIII's supremacy over the Church. The arms of the

Spanish ambassador appear at the bottom right, for his equivalent in the 1620s, Gondomar, lived in Ely Place for a few years. Pope John XXIII's arms appear at the top. The north and south windows of 1952–8 (also by Charles Blakeman) show New and Old Testament scenes respectively, and bear in addition the names and arms of pre-Reformation Bishops of Ely. Between the windows there are sizeable statues of Catholic martyrs of Tudor times, by Mary Blakeman, 1962–4. At the east end, to the right of the altar, there is a gabled reliquary, which contains a portion of St Etheldreda's hand. A statue of the patroness is fixed to the wall above. Another saint whose prayers are invoked here on account of a relic is St Blaise, on whose feast-day (3 February) a blessing is offered as crossed candles are held against the throat.

St George's Bloomsbury

Bloomsbury Way

ABOVE Giant columns and heavy entablatures are the vocabulary of Hawksmoor's internal plan.

OPPOSITE The reredos is seen here restored to its original position in the eastern apse. The 17th-century chandelier is a worthy new addition.

A patron saint, a new monarch and one of the seven wonders of the ancient world are all celebrated in the fabric of St George's, Bloomsbury. It is regarded as one of the most authentically Classical churches in London. Its architect was Nicholas Hawksmoor, whose usual vigorous style produced here a deep portico that has been admired as the most Roman of its type in London, and whose stepped spire is based on Pliny's account of the Mausoleum at Halicarnassus, one of the seven wonders of the ancient world. St George's was built under the Fifty New Churches Act.

The ancient parish out of which St George's was formed was that of St Giles-in-the-Fields. The Bloomsbury portion had developed very rapidly in the later 17th century and had become a decidedly fashionable quarter. The streets and squares of the parish resound today with the names of the nobility. By the time the new church was completed in 1731, the Duke of Bedford and the Duke of Montagu were local residents and vestrymen (or parochial councillors); Sir Hans Sloane, the rich physician and owner of the manor of Chelsea, who was to be the principal founder of the British Museum, lived in Bloomsbury Place (where his house survives); and William Hicks, the royal brewer and Member of Parliament, who paid for the statue of King George I on top of the steeple, was also a vestryman.

The Commissioners of the Fifty New Churches Act began to discuss a church in Bloomsbury in 1714. James Gibbs was directed to survey a site, and both he and Nicholas Hawksmoor were asked to design a church. Then in 1715 Sir John Vanbrugh, the architect of Blenheim Palace and Castle Howard, was asked to make a design: what an extravagance he might have produced! Hawksmoor finally won the day in 1716, and work on his church proceeded from then until 1731.

It is the stepped steeple surmounted by the statue that gives St George's its distinctive frontage. In this case, we do not have a steeple that appears to rest on top of the portico or that stands behind it (as at St Martin-in-the-Fields). The deep portico fronts Bloomsbury Way on

the south and is raised on a flight of steps. The tower is placed instead on the west side, where it does not compete with the portico. The steeple was adorned with lions, unicorns, festoons and crowns until they were removed in 1871, but they were reinstated in 2006. The steeple appears in Hogarth's Gin Lane, dating from 1751. Less familiar to visitors is the church's north front, which is very different from the south portico and yet amounts to an equally impressive Classical composition. It consists of five bays of arched windows and blank arcading in two tiers, the upper divided by Corinthian half-columns, the lower by Corinthian pilasters. The whole is surmounted by a pediment, with one large semicircular motif in the tympanum, and below the lower tier there are huge keystones to the windows of the crypt.

The cost of the church reached about £31,000, inclusive of the rectory. For all its splendour and the high social standing of the district, the site was

cramped, and had a natural north–south axis rather than the usual east–west one. Hawksmoor nevertheless put the altar on the east side. The interior was reordered in 1781 and the principal motive was to increase the number of seats. This reordering was reversed in the recent restoration.

Inside, the plan chiefly features a central square that is higher than the rest and is lit by large clerestory windows. The altar was on the north side until recently, beyond two wide arches that spring from short stretches of entablature, supported by paired columns. The details of these features are gilded. The architecture of the north side looks unduly complicated, given that this side was originally intended to be just a lateral aisle and to be largely obscured by a gallery. On the west side there

RIGHT *A detail of the reredos, the focus of the interior.*

BELOW RIGHT *A graceful staircase, with an arched window in the background.*

is a space beneath the tower, and on the east there is an apse. The reredos was originally placed in this apse, and is now placed there again. The ceiling decoration of the apse (by Isaac Mansfield) not only points to the initial layout by being a mark of honour for an altar, but proves the matter by including a 'pelican in her piety', symbolic of the Eucharist. The reredos that was made for the apse was moved to the north wall in 1781 and has now returned to its old home. The church originally had north and south galleries; the former was the Duke of Montagu's, the latter the Duke of Bedford's. (Servants sat in the tower gallery.) There is still the old south gallery, which until recently housed a 19th-century organ brought from Emmanuel Church, Maida Hill, in 1952. The north gallery is a recent (and unusual) revival. G. E. Street cut down the box-pews and the pulpit in 1871 and moved the pulpit to one side (east of the altar) from its original central position. The paving is new.

The only grand monument stands under the tower and commemorates Charles Grant (died 1823), Chairman of the East India Company and Member of Parliament for Inverness. The East India Company paid for the statue and it was carved by Samuel Manning the elder (1788–1842). Some smaller memorials commemorate officials of the British Museum or their wives: see the tablets to Frederick Madden's wife and son (both died 1830) and to Frances Jane, Lady Ellis (died 1854), the wife of Sir Henry Ellis.

St George's has never looked so splendid since its earliest days: light, spacious and stately.

St Pancras Parish Church
Upper Woburn Place

HISTORY
- Built in 1819–22 by William and Henry William Inwood
- A major Greek Revival design, with details based on Greek Classical buildings

OF SPECIAL INTEREST
- The west portico and tower
- The caryatid porches at the east end
- The giant Ionic columns at the east end, forming a screen
- The organ in the west gallery, with a fine Greek Revival case

The famous railway station that was opened in 1868 took its name from an ancient parish that developed rapidly in Georgian times. A bigger church was needed and the result was a remarkable Greek Revival building, which was built in 1819–22 to the designs of William Inwood and his son, Henry William. Henry William Inwood travelled to Greece to study Classical buildings. In 1827 he published *The Erectheion at Athens*, whose details he had duly copied in Upper Woburn Place.

The church has a west portico of six Ionic columns and a tower that is copied from a Classical Greek building, the Temple of the Winds. The octagonal original is repeated here in three diminishing stages. A short obelisk spire and cross surmount it. The body of the church has two substantial projections at the east angles. These projections each have four draped female figures or caryatides, as at the Erectheion (an original is in the British Museum). They were made of terracotta round an iron spine. The interior preserves its galleries, box-pews, and high Georgian pulpit on Ionic columns. Six giant Ionic columns of scagliola or imitation marble stand in the apse, on a high base and away from the wall, emphasizing the east end. The sanctuary and choir were largely refitted in 1889. Six more Ionic columns support the west gallery, where the organ has a fine Greek Revival case.

ABOVE The tower is based on the Temple of the Winds in Athens, and the caryatid porch is copied from the Erechtheion.

RIGHT The well-preserved late Georgian interior includes a monumental screen of Ionic columns at the east end.

Old Royal Naval College Chapel

King William Walk

HISTORY

- Built in the late 17th century as part of Greenwich Hospital for former mariners of the Royal Navy
- Remodelled in the late 18th century by James 'Athenian' Stuart

OF SPECIAL INTEREST

- The painting by Benjamin West at the east end, which shows St Paul saved from shipwreck on the island of Malta
- The altar of six cherubim in gilded Coade stone
- The pulpit
- The bust of Admiral Sir Thomas Hardy, commander of the *Victory*

ABOVE The domed Queen Mary Block was built by Wren to house the chapel.

RIGHT Pensioners of the Royal Navy were heartened by the painting over the altar of St Paul being saved from shipwreck on Malta, where many of them would have served.

The great palace by the river at Greenwich, which Sir Christopher Wren and other architects built for pensioners of the Royal Navy and which long housed the Royal Naval College, is one of London's most significant buildings. King William III gave the site and existing buildings for use as a Naval Hospital, to match the Royal Hospital for soldiers at Chelsea.

King William's wife and co-monarch gave her name to the Queen Mary Block on the east side, which includes the chapel. The domed tower stands over the chapel's entrance. To its east, there are eight bays with three tiers of windows. This is an interesting variation on the usual two tiers that light a galleried church. Here, the lowest windows light the crypt. The segment-vaulted interior seems markedly tall and wide, for the galleries are narrow and rest on their curved brackets rather high up the walls. The east end has two pairs of huge Corinthian columns in scagliola or imitation marble, and between them an equally huge painting by Benjamin West of St Paul saved from shipwreck on Malta. The altar consists of six cherubim in gilded Coade stone, supporting a marble slab. The pulpit is a handsome work of limewood, mahogany and oak; its circular medallions by West are in Coade stone and show scenes from St Paul's life. Under the west gallery there is a bust of Admiral Sir Thomas Hardy, who commanded the *Victory* at Trafalgar.

St Alfege
Greenwich Church Street

HISTORY

- Built in 1712–18 by Nicholas Hawksmoor on the site of an ancient church
- The steeple was added in 1730 by John James
- One of the Fifty New Churches: the one that prompted the entire group
- Named after the Archbishop of Canterbury who was martyred at Greenwich in 1012
- General James Wolfe, the conqueror of Quebec, was buried here in 1759
- General Charles Gordon, who fell at Khartoum, was baptized here in 1833

OF SPECIAL INTEREST

- The east façade to Greenwich Church Street
- The *trompe l'oeil* painting at the east end
- The emblems of the royal pew in the west gallery
- The figure of Cardinal Morton in the east window, and in a vestibule window
- The charities' boards, which list an unusually significant group of charities

OPPOSITE *Hawksmoor's impressive south elevation is divided by giant pillasters. James's steeple, seen beyond, was added to the original tower in 1730.*

It is a rare church in England, let alone London, that can claim to be built on the site of the martyrdom of the saint after whom it is named. In this case, St Alfege was martyred at Greenwich by the Vikings on 9 April 1012. A slab in the pavement of the chancel commemorates the event. St Alfege had been Archbishop of Canterbury since 1006, and his remains were eventually enshrined in his cathedral. St Alfege's Church has countless further associations. In its parish a royal palace stood for a couple of centuries and as a result, King Henry VIII was baptized in the parish. His sister, Mary Tudor, married Charles Brandon, Duke of Suffolk, in the palace's chapel in 1515. From later centuries, two British imperial heroes are associated with the church. General James Wolfe, the conqueror of Quebec (died 1759) was buried here and is commemorated by a tablet of 1908; his victory was one of those in the *annus mirabilis* of 1759, which prompted David Garrick to write *Heart of Oak*. The other hero is General Charles Gordon (died 1885), the Victorian soldier who fell at Khartoum in the Sudan. He was baptized here in 1833. A lesser known but very worthy commemoration is that of Canon John Miller, a Victorian Rector of St Alfege's, who helped to found Hospital Sunday. This was a valuable means of supporting voluntary hospitals before the National Health Service.

St Alfege's was built in 1712–18 by Nicholas Hawksmoor. John James encased the surviving tower from the previous church in 1730, and added a steeple. The church was rebuilt under the 1711 Act. In fact, it had a prominent position in the Fifty New Churches scheme, because it was a petition from Greenwich in 1711, asking that money from the coal dues be granted for rebuilding the storm-damaged St Alfege's, that led to the Act in the first place. The church was bombed in 1941, and had the privilege of restoration by Sir Albert Richardson. Few architects in the 20th century were so wedded to the Georgian Age as he was; he even went about by sedan chair in his home town of Ampthill in Bedfordshire.

The tower and steeple of St Alfege's are designed after the manner of James Gibbs: worthy and pleasing, but unlike Hawksmoor's much

more vigorous architecture in the body of the church. The east end faces the centre of Greenwich, and it is that elevation that makes the most dramatic statement. A pediment surmounted by three huge urns crowns the whole, which is divided by four Doric pilasters at the sides and two columns in the middle; the columns frame the recessed east window, above which an arch breaks through into the pediment itself. The side elevations of nine bays are also divided by giant pilasters. The three middle bays project considerably to provide vestibules for north and south doors. Urns surmount the west end of the church proper, as at the east.

The post-war interior reproduces Hawksmoor's design and the fittings of the craftsmen who worked with him. The east apse is framed by a shallow arch and by pilasters that still bear monochrome painting of the 18th century by Sir James Thornhill. The painting he executed in the apse itself was redone after the Second World War by Glyn Jones. The half-dome is made to appear coffered. The east window is flanked by pairs of giant Corinthian columns, set diagonally towards the centre; they support short entablatures only, although they appear to support the arch of the window, for the dark woodwork seems to merge into the dark *trompe l'oeil* painting. The reredos proper consists of four small, evenly spaced Corinthian columns and a straight entablature, immediately under the east window. The stained glass in the window was designed by Ruskin Spear, 1953, and shows the Risen Christ accompanied by four angels holding Instruments of the Passion. Small figures of St Alfege and Cardinal Morton appear at the bottom. Cardinal Morton, who served as Archbishop of Canterbury, was Vicar here from 1444 to 1454. He also appears in a window in the vestibule, which was the only 19th-century window in the church to survive the bombing of 1941. Ruskin Spear also designed the aisle windows in 1956. They represent historical scenes of the church and parish. One worthy not mentioned above but who is commemorated here is Thomas Tallis. He was buried in the previous church and might have known the organ console in the gallery, at least part of which is thought to go back to 1552. He is shown in a south aisle window, at the west end. The Stuart royal arms are placed in the west gallery to represent the church's traditional royal pew.

The benefaction boards at the east end list an extraordinary group of charities. Greenwich has seemingly been blessed with benevolence beyond any other parish. The Royal Hospital for mariners takes pride of place: its premises constituted a palace. The others include Trinity Hospital at the waterfront, a charming almshouse founded by the Earl of Northampton in 1613; the Roan School; Queen Elizabeth's College, also an almshouse, which stands opposite Greenwich Station; and the Jubilee Almshouses in Greenwich High Road. The scale and number of this parish's charities are remarkable.

St Nicholas's

Deptford Green

Deptford is steeped in English maritime history. Rotherhithe, Deptford and Greenwich were all chiefly known in past centuries for their maritime connections, but of the three, Deptford was by far the most important. It was the site of a royal dockyard from 1513 to 1869. Many eminent naval men lived there, as their successors would tend to live near Portsmouth or Devonport. Lord Howard of Effingham, the commander against the Spanish Armada, lived at Deptford Green. His deputy, Sir Francis Drake, received his knighthood from Queen Elizabeth I at Deptford in 1581, after returning from his circumnavigation. Sir John Hawkins at one time lived in the house of the Navy's Treasurer at Deptford. In 1638 another Treasurer paid to have the chancel of St Nicholas's Church extended.

Just a year after the royal dockyard was founded, there was established at Deptford the corporation of Trinity House, which still looks after lighthouses and lightships. The corporation's splendid full title is the 'Fraternity of the Master, Wardens and Assistants of the Guild or Fraternity of the Most Glorious and Undivided Trinity and of St Nicholas in the Parish Church of Deptford Strond in the County of Kent'. The parish church of

RIGHT The late mediaeval tower survived the rebuilding of the church by Charley Stanton in 1697. His is the south elevation seen here, surmounted by a Dutch gable.

OPPOSITE The Jacobean pulpit predates the remainder of the furnishings.

Deptford Strond is, of course, St Nicholas's. Trinity House's property at Deptford used to stand east of the church. Since 1795 its headquarters have been in the familiar building at Tower Hill.

The Honourable East India Company, another pillar of England's maritime history, also had significant connections with Deptford. Many of the company's ships were built here, including the four that sailed on the company's first voyage in 1601. The Governor of the company lived at Deptford. In 1640 a north aisle was added to (old) St Nicholas's, mainly at the company's expense.

The major landed estate of the parish was that of Sayes Court, made famous as the home of John Evelyn. Towards the end of the 17th century, however, the mansion was rented to Admiral Benbow, and after him (in 1698) to Tsar Peter the Great, who had come to Deptford to study shipbuilding. The Tsar swiftly earned the reputation locally of a ruffian. He would have found congenial company a century earlier in Christopher Marlowe, the Elizabethan dramatist, who was murdered in a Deptford tavern and who is buried at St Nicholas's. There is a modern tablet commemorating him in the church.

In 1730 the ancient parish of St Nicholas was divided. The old church kept the heart of Deptford by the Thames and the rest was handed over to the new parish of St Paul. In 1900, the parish of St Nicholas was placed in the new Metropolitan Borough of Greenwich, whereas St Paul's was placed in that of Deptford. St Nicholas's, therefore, was no longer in what one might properly term its own borough: a curious situation.

The church we see today largely dates from a rebuilding of 1697 by Charley Stanton. It is of red brick with stone dressings. The exception is the tower of Kentish ragstone, which has survived from the late Middle Ages. Its upper part was rebuilt by George Parker in 1903–4. The church was bombed and gutted in the Blitz. Restoration by Thomas F Ford and Partners was completed in 1958. Charley Stanton was also reponsible for the rebuilding of St Mary Magdalen's, Bermondsey. The plans of the two churches are similar. In this case, Stanton provided a nave of four bays, divided from wide aisles by Tuscan arcades. A crossing was provided in the second bay from the west by turning the entablatures towards the north and south walls, and although the transepts

LEFT *The view towards the reredos, a furnishing which is closely comparable to those in Wren's City churches.*

RIGHT *Down to the 19th century it was usual to see the Commandments inscribed on the altarpiece, and for the latter to incorporate paintings of Moses and Aaron (seen here).*

thus created do not project beyond the aisles, they are given much emphasis externally, as at Bermondsey. The big Dutch gable familiar from many pictures of the south side of the church is considered old-fashioned for a building of 1697. Within the church, there is a groined vault over the crossing. The nave and transepts have elliptical vaults. The east end formerly had a shallow chancel, but after the war the east bay of the nave was screened off, making the remainder square and symmetrical. At one time there were galleries to north, south and west, as at Bermondsey, but the galleries over the aisles were removed long ago and the west one (with its original organ case) was ruined in the bombing. The present arrangements are postwar.

The 17th-century fittings were rescued from the wartime ruins. The pulpit is Jacobean (with fine carving on its panels and a fine staircase), but the other fittings are contemporary with the building of the church. The reredos and its associated panelling were formerly placed against the three walls of the original chancel, but now they are flattened out, so to speak, against the present east wall. The reredos incorporates paintings of Moses and Aaron, and carved figures of St John the Evangelist and a prophet, perhaps Isaiah. The ensemble is closely comparable with work in Wren's City churches. To the right there is a carving of Ezekiel's vision, which was once placed over the entrance to the Charnel House in the churchyard. This carving and the reredos have been ascribed to Grinling Gibbons, who lived in Deptford, but it is generally thought unlikely that he carved them. The

communion table and chairs are 17th-century but new to the church in the postwar restoration. To the left of the reredos there is a copy of Kneller's picture of Queen Anne, which had been intended for St Paul's, Deptford, upon its opening in 1730. King William III's arms were replaced in 1958.

The naval memorials once led to the church's being called 'the Westminster Abbey of the Navy'. Some were destroyed in the Second World War, but a good selection survives. On the north wall there is a memorial to Peter Pett (died 1652), who is credited with the introduction of the frigate and was the nephew of Phineas Pett, who designed the *Sovereign of the Seas* (1637). On the opposite wall another memorial commemorates Jonas Shish (died 1680), equally eminent as a shipbuilder. An earlier memorial that has often been remarked commemorates Roger Boyle and Edward Fenton. Boyle was a schoolboy and the eldest son of the first Earl of Cork, who died when he was at school at Deptford. His younger brothers included the first Earl of Burlington and Robert Boyle, the physicist. Edward Fenton was the uncle of the Earl of Cork's wife. He was an Elizabethan naval commander who sailed with Frobisher and who commanded the *Mary Rose* against the Armada (not the same *Mary Rose* that is at Portsmouth). He died in 1603. The joint memorial dates from after 1620 and was designed by Epiphanius Evesham. Near the altar there is a stone to John Benbow, the son of the admiral who lodged at Sayes Court. One memorial remains of a group that once recalled members of John Evelyn's family. It commemorates his children, Richard and Elizabeth.

Wesley's Chapel

City Road

HISTORY

- Built in 1777–8 by George Dance the younger to replace the Foundery Chapel of 1739
- The principal chapel of John Wesley, the founder of Methodism
- Reordered and embellished in the 19th century
- Much restored in recent years

OF SPECIAL INTEREST

- Statue of John Wesley in the courtyard by J. Adams-Acton
- The central pulpit, from which the Methodist pioneers preached
- Memorials of distinguished Methodists over the past two centuries
- The Foundery chapel south of the main chapel
- John Wesley's tomb at the rear of the chapel
- The Museum of Methodism in the crypt

ABOVE RIGHT John Wesley's tomb (right) at the rear of the chapel, with the chapel itself reflected in the glass of the adjoining offices.

John Wesley (1703–91) was one of the greatest figures in English Christian history, for he founded and led the huge new movement of Methodism, and throughout his adult life travelled and preached all over England and also in North America. He was the son of an Anglican parson, and his rescue from fire as a child made him think that he had a special destiny. The text, 'A brand plucked out of the burning', featured many times in his diary. He was ordained in the Church of England, but not until he underwent a further religious conversion in 1738 did his great mission begin. 'I felt my heart strangely warmed,' he wrote after a meeting in Aldersgate near the present Museum of London. In 1739 he bought an old workshop in City Road and converted it into the Foundery Chapel. It lasted until the present Wesley's Chapel was built in 1777–8.

George Dance the younger designed the chapel. Since his day it has acquired a portico (in 1815) and vestibule wings, and it has required much restoration. But its appearance is not very different to that of 1778. Its façade, set well back behind a courtyard dominated by a statue of Wesley by J. Adams-Acton, 1891, is of five bays, of which the middle

BELOW LEFT *The statue of John Wesley by J. Adams-Acton seen with the chapel's principal façade in the background.*

BELOW RIGHT *The pulpit and the gallery are Georgian, but the jasper columns and the stained glass are late Victorian embellishments.*

three project slightly and are surmounted by a pediment. The chapel has a wide, galleried interior, with an east recess for the Classical reredos and altar, and a screened vestibule on the west wide. The fittings and adornments have grown in number and richness since the 18th century. The polished Jasper columns that support the gallery replaced wooden ships' masts donated by King George III, some of which can now be seen in the vestibule. The pews were replaced in 1891. The pulpit still stands in the middle, as in a pre-Victorian Anglican church, but it is only the top section of the original three-decker. John Wesley's well-known brother Charles, preached from it with energetic gesticulations. On one occasion, he knocked a hymn-book onto the head of a prayer-reader in a lower tier. When the pulpit Bible fell a little later, the reader was ready to catch it, to the congregation's amusement. Charles Wesley was a celebrated writer of hymns. His chamber organ is kept in the Foundery chapel, a small, top-lit room that stands south of the chapel proper.

John Wesley's tomb is located to the rear of the chapel. An urn surmounts a monument of three receding stages, with long inscriptions which record Wesley's extraordinary mission. The Museum of Methodism which was opened in the chapel's crypt in 1984 tells of that mission's results over two and a half centuries.

London Oratory
Brompton Road

OPPOSITE *The substantial sanctuary has a modest canopy over the high altar rather than the intended baldacchino. The two seven-branched candlesticks were given by the Marquess of Bute. On the right there may be seen two of the 17th-century Apostles' statues from Siena.*

The Congregation of the Oratory was founded in Rome by St Philip Neri (1515–95) as part of the renewal of the Roman Catholic Church after the Reformation. The Oratory was brought into England in 1848 by Cardinal Newman (1801–90), but he settled in Birmingham, and it was therefore his fellow convert from the Church of England, Frederick William Faber (1814–63), who set up the London Oratory in South Kensington. The district is so firmly a part of central London today that it is difficult to credit Faber's description of it in the early 1850s as 'the Madeira of London', but at that time Kensington Gardens could be seen from the house. A temporary church by J. J. Scoles was ready by 1854. It was not until 1880–4 that the great Italianate church we know today was built to the designs of Herbert Gribble, and only in 1893–6 were the familiar west front and dome added. By then, the cost had exceeded £100,000. Herbert Gribble (1847–94) had worked with J. A. Hansom, who had designed the great Gothic church of St Philip Neri at Arundel in Sussex for the 15th Duke of Norfolk. The Duke gave £20,000 to the London Oratory, and it is thought that his influence helped to secure the commission at Brompton for Gribble.

The principal façade has a lower storey that is brought forward from the nave to create a narthex and that also embraces the single-storey aisles. Gribble originally intended flanking towers, but they were never built. The entrance features four pairs of Corinthian columns and pilasters with a balustraded parapet above. The pedimented nave is surmounted by a statue of the Virgin Mary, and has the arms of St Philip Neri in the tympanum. The transepts reach to the same height as the nave, forming a Latin Cross, which is domed at the crossing. The dome was supervised by George Sherrin, but it is thought that his assistant, Edwin Rickards, was its main designer. The dome is taller than Gribble had intended, but as a result it is easier to see from Brompton Road. A memorial to Cardinal Newman by Farmer & Brindley stands to the west of the entrance, incorporating a statue by L. J. Chavalliaud.

The broad nave is three bays long, and each bay is flanked by side chapels set at right angles to it. Pairs of giant Corinthian pilasters in Plymouth marble articulate the nave; pairs of much smaller Corinthian columns support the arches into the chapels. Between the pilasters there are statues of the Apostles, carved by Giuseppe Mazzuoli between 1679 and 1695, which once stood in Siena Cathedral. On the left-hand side, near the crossing, there stands Commendatore Formilli's pulpit of 1930, with a substantial carved tester and a staircase on each side. The crossing is flanked by the Lady chapel on the right and the chapel of St Philip on the left. The Lady altar, a towering Classical composition, is also an old Italian work, for it was made in 1693 for the chapel of the Rosary in the Dominican church at Brescia. For that reason, it features statues of four Dominican saints, but the central statue of Our Lady of Victories came from the first London Oratory near the Strand. Gribble himself designed St Philip's

altar, which was the gift of the 15th Duke of Norfolk. A wax effigy of the saint lies beneath the altar. For the high altar, Gribble had intended a baldacchino such as the one we see at Westminster Cathedral, but this plan was not carried out, and instead there is a modest canopy. A painting of a scene from St Philip's life stands behind the altar, and two more fill the side arches of the sanctuary. In the south-east corner of the church there is a large additional chapel of St Wilfrid, whose high altar is an 18th-century work from the church of St Remy at Rochefort, Belgium. Father Faber's grave lies in front of the altar, with a Latin inscription on the stone; St Wilfrid was his chosen patron. In the same chapel, the altar of the English Martyrs has above it a triptych by Rex Whistler, 1938, which depicts Thomas More and John Fisher, who were then newly canonized. The shrine of St Cecilia, also in this chapel, has an effigy that copies the one by Stefano Maderno in her church in Rome.

FAR LEFT The organ gallery, which houses the instrument completed in 1954 to Ralph Downes's design.

LEFT The Lady altar was made for the Dominican church at Brescia in Italy in 1693, but the central statue of the Virgin Mary came from the first London Oratory near the Strand.

RIGHT A view from the south-west corner of the church towards the Lady chapel, across the various side-chapels. A First World War memorial featuring a white marble pieta stands under the arch on the left.

BELOW Rex Whistler's altarpiece of the English Martyrs in St Wilfrid's chapel, 1938, showing St Thomas More (left), St John Fisher (right) and executions at Tyburn (centre). More and Fisher had been canonized in 1935.

The organ was designed by Ralph Downes and built by J. W. Walker & Sons in 1954. The church has a distinguished musical tradition, which is one of the features that ensures the Oratory a significant place in the life of the Catholic Church in London.

St Mary Abbots
Kensington Church Street

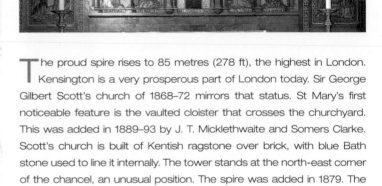

HISTORY
- Built in 1869–72 by Sir George Gilbert Scott on the site of an old church
- The cloister in the churchyard was added in 1889–93 by J. T. Micklethwaite and Somers Clarke
- A major Victorian church in the Early English style, with a spire rising to 85 metres (278 ft)

OF SPECIAL INTEREST
- Scott's reredos
- The monument to the seventh Earl of Warwick by J. B. Guelfi
- The pulpit given by King William III
- The remains of the monument to William Courten, carved by Grinling Gibbons and given by Sir Hans Sloane

ABOVE The arcade in Early English style.

ABOVE RIGHT Scott's reredos, the focus of the interior.

The proud spire rises to 85 metres (278 ft), the highest in London. Kensington is a very prosperous part of London today. Sir George Gilbert Scott's church of 1868–72 mirrors that status. St Mary's first noticeable feature is the vaulted cloister that crosses the churchyard. This was added in 1889–93 by J. T. Micklethwaite and Somers Clarke. Scott's church is built of Kentish ragstone over brick, with blue Bath stone used to line it internally. The tower stands at the north-east corner of the chancel, an unusual position. The spire was added in 1879. The style of the church is 13th-century Geometrical, which Scott generally deployed, but rarely did he have the chance to build so lavish a church.

The interior, 54.5 metres (179 ft) long, focuses on the high altar and reredos, which Scott designed and the firm of Clayton & Bell made. Clayton & Bell also provided most of the stained glass. An exception is the east window of the chapel of the Resurrection, which is by James Powell. The pulpit is a panelled and finely moulded Classical example that was given in 1697 by King William III, the builder of Kensington Palace. The grandest memorial (in the south transept) is ascribed to J. B. Guelfi and commemorates the seventh Earl of Warwick (died 1721). The Earl sits languidly in Roman dress and leans on an urn, against a large pedimented backplate surmounted by his arms. An earlier monument, to William Courten (died 1702), has distinguished connections, for it was carved by Grinling Gibbons for Sir Hans Sloane.

St Mary-at-Lambeth

Lambeth Palace Road

ABOVE The pedlar, who traditionally gave an acre of land to the parish on the site of County Hall (access on application).

RIGHT Captain Bligh's tomb in the churchyard.

St Mary's has been run since 1979 by the Tradescant Trust as the Garden Museum, for in its churchyard there lie buried those famous pioneers of English horticulture, John Tradescant (*c*.1570–1638) and his son, also John (1608–62), gardeners to the monarchs and magnates of Stuart England. West of their tomb stands the monument of William Bligh, who was the master of the *Bounty* in 1789 when the notorious mutiny took place. His house still stands in Lambeth Road.

The church is a remodelling by P. C. Hardwick in 1851–2 of a building of 1374–7, whose aisles were rebuilt and extended in early Tudor times. Its architectural character is therefore that of 14th-century Decorated. Lambeth Palace stands next door as the London home of the Archbishops of Canterbury; the palace's 15th-century red-brick gateway forms a picturesque pair with St Mary's ragstone tower. Several archbishops have been buried in the church, or have memorials there.

The interior walls and columns are very sprucely cleaned amidst the museum's display. The tall nave has standard 14th-century octagonal columns with moulded capitals. The sizeable chancel has two Tudor tomb-chests, flanking the former high altar, but now hidden behind a screen. The east window has flowing tracery and is filled with stained glass by Francis Stevens. The west window is Perpendicular and has stained glass in memory of Archbishop Moore. On the north wall there is a terracotta carving of the Crucifixion by George Tinworth.

St Paul's Church

Diamond Way, off Deptford High Street

HISTORY

- Built in 1713–30 by Thomas Archer
- One of the Fifty New Churches
- One of London's foremost Baroque churches
- Scene of the distinguished ministry of Canon David Diamond, Rector, 1969–92

OF SPECIAL INTEREST

- West portico and tower
- 18th-century pulpit with iron stairs
- Venetian east window and altar screen
- Memorial to Dr Charles Burney, Rector and brother of Fanny Burney, the novelist

ABOVE A graceful 18th-century wooden staircase.

OPPOSITE Thomas Archer's exuberant Baroque church skilfully combines a west tower with a sizeable portico.

Sir John Betjeman once called this church 'a pearl in the heart of Deptford'. It is an exuberant Baroque building in Portland stone, which was designed by Thomas Archer and built in 1713–30 under the Fifty New Churches Act. The old maritime district it serves has been much battered by redevelopment and war, and it was the setting of an immense pastoral effort by the late Canon David Diamond, Rector from 1969 to 1992. He was a fierce critic of post-war planners, for he saw their work as producing social disintegration. He thought that the Church should lead in picking up the pieces. He wanted to make St Paul's not only a precious architectural symbol of Deptford, but also the focus of local life. His remarkable ministry saw the church restored and its mission made as vibrant and expansive as any in London. Even the Millwall football team joined in.

The church is raised on a platform and is almost square. Its principal or west front has a semicircular, balustraded portico of four Tuscan columns standing in front of a circular tower. This arrangement is eminently successful in combining a Classical portico with a tall, English steeple, and it is often contrasted favourably with Gibbs's design at St Martin-in-the-Fields. Thomas Archer had visited Rome, where he presumably knew Pietro da Cortona's church of St Maria della Pace, and so he might have used a semicircular portico independently of Wren's examples in St Paul's Cathedral.

There is an east apse to mirror the portico. On the north and south sides there are pediments that surmount the three projecting middle bays. Tall, arched windows with prominent keystones are divided by rusticated Tuscan pilasters. There are double staircases leading to north and south doors: a feature that one would normally associate more with the terrace of a country house than a church.

As in many 17th- and 18th-century churches, there is an ambivalence in the internal plan. It appears to be square, and the filling-in of the corners for staircases and vestries makes it approximate to a Greek cross. Moreover, the corners are canted to the nave, which helps to give the impression of a centralized plan. On the other hand, two Corinthian

LEFT The east end in 1999. After a fire in 2000, the church was redecorated as it was in 1723. Clear glass has replaced the stained glass in the curving Venetian window, and the gilding and the communion rails have gone.

BELOW LEFT The semicircular portico ultimately derives from the church of St Maria della Pace at Rome.

BELOW RIGHT The interior facing the organ gallery, showing one of the giant Corinthian columns that divide the interior. The font has since been moved from in front of the door.

columns mark off the north and south sides as aisles, for the entablature they carry runs from east to west and is not diverted to indicate transepts. The aisles also house galleries to add to the longitudinal effect, and the apse draws attention to the traditional east altar. The Venetian east window curves round the apse and fits into a screen that terminates in a column at each end; a decidedly Baroque arrangement.

The fine 18th-century pulpit has iron stairs. As usual, it is only one part of a former three-decker. The font, however, is not a Georgian original but a late Victorian import from Rochester Cathedral and is incongruously neo-Norman in style. Among the memorials there is one to Dr Charles Burney, Rector from 1811 to 1817, who was the brother of the greatly admired novelist Fanny Burney.

Southwark Cathedral
London Bridge

OPPOSITE *The 13th-century choir, which has been embellished over the past hundred years.*

ew acres of London have had so eventful a past as those that make up the ancient town of Southwark. The town's *raison d'être* was London Bridge, which was London's only bridge from Roman times until as recently as 1750. Southwark was London's gateway from the south. The cathedral has stood sentinel over this southern approach for over a thousand years. Chaucer's pilgrims, Shakespeare's plays, the mediaeval rebellions of Wat Tyler and Jack Cade, and the mediaeval palace of the powerful Bishops of Winchester have all been part of the story of its ancient parish.

William Shakespeare's Globe Theatre once stood in the cathedral's parish, and Shakespeare's brother Edmund, an actor, was buried in the church in 1607 'with a forenoone knell of the great bell'. The playwright himself has a substantial 20th-century memorial. The cathedral's records show that many of his actors lived in the surrounding streets; the first Hamlet, for example – Joseph Taylor – lived in Langley's Rents off Park Street. In the same year in which Edmund Shakespeare was buried in the church, John Harvard, the founder of the American university, was baptized in it. The great Tabard Inn, from which Chaucer's Canterbury pilgrims set out in the 14th century, was also in the parish; Chaucer's contemporary, the poet John Gower, is commemorated in the cathedral by its most striking mediaeval monument. In fact, the cathedral has monuments of great interest in abundance, including those of a saintly Jacobean bishop (Lancelot Andrewes), a City Alderman of the same era (Richard Humble) and a physician (Lionel Lockyer), whose cure-all pills made him famous in King Charles II's time.

Southwark was probably founded as a fortified town or *burh* as a defence against the Vikings, possibly in King Alfred's time in the late 9th century. Its ancient name, *Suthringa geweorche* ('the defensive work of the men of Surrey'), makes it clear that it was a *burh*. *Burhs* generally had a church, and it is likely that Southwark Cathedral originated in that way. Only archaeology will tell its early history in more detail. The cathedral first appears in written history in the Domesday Book (1086),

which describes it as a minster, and states that it was then in the hands of Odo, Bishop of Bayeux in Normandy. A minster was more important than an ordinary parish church: it was the chief church of a district or one whose history or possessions marked it out as being special.

Southwark's minster was made the church of an Augustinian priory in the early 12th century. The priory had the name of St Mary Overy, whose 'surname' means either 'over the river' or 'on the bank'. William Gifford, Bishop of Winchester, was possibly the priory's founder. From a little later in the 12th century, when the mighty Henry of Blois – King Stephen's brother – was Bishop of Winchester, the bishops lived in a palace next door to the priory. Ruins of it survive today.

The building we see today dates from between the 13th and the 15th centuries and from the late 19th century (a period of intense restoration), with minor contributions from other eras. The mediaeval glory of the building is the 13th-century choir, whose date is reflected in dog-tooth moulding and in the characteristic shapes of piers and arches. The overall design is generally stated to show French influence. The vaulting shafts go right down to the ground; there is an arcaded wall-passage rather than a normal triforium; and the vaults are quadripartite. All these features were more French than English in the period at issue. In the 19th century, the clerestory and vaults were rebuilt by George Gwilt the younger, who also replaced the east window. The choir is of five bays. Behind it is the retrochoir, which has three bays spanning the full width of the choir and its aisles. It is divided on its east side into four chapels, which correspond with the four small gables seen from the approach to London Bridge. The retrochoir is also 13th-century in character, but with just a little later detail.

The transepts differ from the predominant character of the building. The north transept appears to have the main surviving Norman fabric: rubble walling on the north side (seen from outside) and the remains of an east apse in what is now the Harvard Chapel. To the west, in the north nave aisle, there are parts of two doorways that survive from the Norman church: the prior's doorway nearer the transept, and the canons' doorway towards the west end. The south transept shows 14th-century work in its windows. It also has a cast of the arms of Cardinal Beaufort, Bishop of Winchester, on its east side. This might indicate work he had undertaken in the chapel that once stood east of the transept. He might also have had a connection with the building of the tower, which is of 14th- and 15th-century date.

The mediaeval nave was cleared away in 1838, but its roof bosses of 1469 survive. Sir Arthur Blomfield designed the present seven-bay nave in 1890–7. Its design is based on the 13th-century choir, but adds a few embellishments. It is a very worthy contribution to the whole and serves to remind us of the huge and costly effort that the Victorians put into the care of churches. In effect, all the works from 1890 to 1905 were undertaken to make the old church into a cathedral. Woodwork, stained glass, font, organ and memorials were all inserted or renewed as well as a new nave being built. The works between 1890 and the First World War gave the cathedral much of its present character.

Southwark Cathedral is rich in monuments. The oldest is a cross-legged knight from the later 13th century, which may represent one of the family of de Warenne, Earls of Surrey, whose members were benefactors to the priory. The main interest is that this is a wooden effigy, a comparatively rare class. From the 15th century, there survives in the north nave aisle the monument of John Gower, a poet, who lived in the priory's precinct until his death in 1408. His head rests on his three books, which were written in Latin, French and Middle English respectively. The Tudor and Stuart periods are well represented. This was a time of some prosperity and civic pride. It was also the time of the Bankside theatres, including the Globe. Shakespeare's memorial in the south nave aisle dates only from 1912 (by H. W. McCarthy) and the window above is as recent as 1954 (by Christopher Webb). The effigy reclines in front of a panorama of Southwark, with the Globe clearly seen.

BELOW Pugin's tabernacle in the Harvard Chapel, brought here from Pugin's own church at Ramsgate, to Southwark's great advantage.

RIGHT A skewed arch betrays different building campaigns.

FAR RIGHT The north transept.

The grandest of the Tudor and Stuart monuments flank the choir. On the north side there is a memorial to Alderman Richard Humble (died 1616) and his two wives, all kneeling under coffered arches and wearing huge ruffs. The design is attributed to William Cure II, one of the local group of sculptors sometimes known as the Southwark School. On the other side of the choir there is the monument to Lancelot Andrewes, Bishop of Winchester (died 1626), who was the last bishop to live in the palace next door. His many writings still have a readership today. Sir Ninian Comper gave the monument a worthy new canopy in 1930. To the west of it there is a modern memorial by Cecil Thomas to Edward Talbot, the first Bishop of Southwark. It is a very dignified addition, dating from the twentieth century.

Further notable early memorials are these: in the north choir aisle, to John Trehearne (died 1618), 'Gentleman Portar to James I', and his wife; in the north transept, Nicholas Stone's so-called Austin monument, which was erected in 1633 by William Austin for his mother, Lady Clerke, and which has an allegorical theme in agricultural dress; in the same transept, to Lionel Lockyer (died 1672), the inventor of a famous (but dubious) pill that promised to 'vanquish all manner of distempers'; and in the south transept, monuments to William Emerson (died 1575) and John Bingham (died 1625). Outside the south transept a later monument of note is that to George Gwilt the younger (died 1856), whose exertions saved and restored much of the surviving mediaeval fabric of the church.

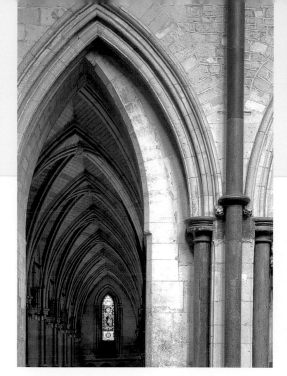

The stained glass of the great west window is Henry Holiday's. C. E. Kempe's firm originally filled the windows of the nave aisles: those on the north side remain, but those on the south were blown out in the Second World War. Sir Ninian Comper designed the glass for the east window of the choir: another post-war replacement. Ward and Hughes designed the martyrs' window at the east end of the north wall in the retrochoir. A window in the Harvard Chapel was made by John Lafarge, an American artist, as part of the 300th anniversary celebrations for John Harvard.

The treasure of the Harvard Chapel is the tall, gilded tabernacle by A. W. N. Pugin. Southwark Cathedral is very fortunate to have such a fine piece. From a later period comes G. F. Bodley's font and cover, but the latter has regrettably been strung up in an unseemly fashion on a metal frame. Bodley also contributed some woodwork in the choir. The great chandelier under the crossing dates from 1689. The stone screen behind the high altar was given by Richard Fox, Bishop of Winchester, in 1520. All the statues are modern. Gilding was introduced earlier this century by Comper. He was also responsible for the furnishings of the altars in the retrochoir; his usual riddel posts and angels abound.

Just south of the crossing there is a more recent memorial to the Bohemian (i.e. Czech) artist, Wenceslaus Hollar (died 1677), who completed his famous panorama of London at about the same time the Civil War erupted in 1642. Only the tower of St Saviour's could have provided such a perfect platform for what proved the most accurate depiction of London before the Great Fire destroyed its mediaeval profile forever.

The recent Chapter House and ancillary buildings, which were opened in 1988, were by Ronald Sims. The work is unsympathetic in style to the Gothic cathedral, even if it tries a little in the choice of materials. Further buildings to more agreeable designs by Richard Griffiths have since been erected on the north side.

St George's Cathedral
Lambeth Road

OPPOSITE Romilly Craze made a true cathedral of St George's in his post-war rebuilding by giving it extra height.

St George's Cathedral is an interesting Gothic work built by Romilly Craze in 1953–8. It is also a restoration of A. W. N. Pugin's bombed church of 1840–8. Pugin was the most forceful propagandist of the Gothic Revival in the first half of the 19th century. When he married his third wife, Jane Knill, at St George's in 1848, he even said that he had at last found a Gothic woman, meaning that she shared his mediaevalist passion. He had immense capabilities, but lacked commensurate opportunities. Here at St George's, want of money stopped his original design, and even the second, less ambitious scheme was never accorded its tower and spire and could not even be given a clerestory. His church was built as a parish church, not as a cathedral, and it must be said that its nave and chancel were not of cathedral size. Craze's post-war nave is certainly worthy of a cathedral – a great improvement on what it replaced – but he did not match Pugin's command of mediaeval detail.

It is a great irony of history that this Catholic cathedral stands on part of St George's Fields, where Lord George Gordon's meeting of the Protestant Association in 1780 prompted the Gordon Riots against Roman Catholics. The church that was started in 1840 replaced a small chapel in nearby London Road and represented a mission that had been founded as early as 1786. So the church was an old foundation in modern Roman Catholic terms. In the 19th century it was also of greater Catholic significance in London, because there was no Westminster Cathedral until 1903. The first head of the revived Catholic hierarchy, Cardinal Wiseman, was enthroned in St George's in 1850 and lived briefly in its clergy house.

Thomas Doyle was the founder of the cathedral. He was a priest in the London Road Chapel from 1820. Between 1852 and his death in 1879 he was Provost of the Chapter. His achievement was considerable, for the congregation was largely a poor one. Pugin became the architect at the insistence of the Earl of Shrewsbury, a Catholic grandee of the time. At the opening in 1848, the Earl collected the offertory, with the Earl of Arundel, from among a very grand

gathering. The Archbishop of Paris could not attend because of the revolution in Paris; a few days later he was dead, having been shot in the street.

The cathedral is 75 metres (247 ft) long and is built of yellow Sussex brick and Portland stone dressings. The west tower, which Craze intended to rise to 56 metres (183 ft), remains a stump. The interior is markedly light and spacious, for Craze's tall nave *does* possess a clerestory, and there is comparatively little stained glass. The nave is impressive architecturally but it is very plain. A vault was intended, but economy led to the use of transverse stone arches with a boarded ceiling in between. The ceiling's eight bays are decorated with symbols of biblical scenes from the Creation to the Passion. All the interesting fittings and adornments are towards the east end. The Blessed Sacrament chapel at the east end of the north aisle still has Pugin's fittings: the altar, reredos, tiles and gates. Their survival is fortunate and surprising. Of particular note are the two chantry chapels. The Knill Chantry stands in the north aisle and is the finest work in the cathedral. It was designed by Edward Pugin after his father's death and was opened in 1857. It is a low, vaulted chapel with an openwork screen to the aisle. Just to the west of it, a stained-glass window by Goddard & Gibbs commemorates Pope John Paul II's visit to the cathedral in 1982. He came to anoint the sick, and that is the theme of the window. In the same aisle there are the monuments to Thomas Doyle, the founder (died 1879), and Archbishop Peter Amigo (died 1949). They both consist of a recumbent effigy on a table-tomb, but in Provost Doyle's case the decorative detail is far more substantial. His monument stands in an arched recess. Archbishop Amigo was Bishop of Southwark for 45 years and was much loved by his flock. He suffered the torment of seeing his cathedral in ruins in 1941. His one appearance on the national stage came in 1920 when he attracted widespread criticism, including some from English Catholics, for his indulgence of an Irish nationalist in the troubles of Lloyd George's time. As a Gibraltarian, Amigo might have been expected to be a robust British patriot, but his flock was largely of Irish origin.

The Petre Chantry by A. W. N. Pugin, 1848–9, is a small vaulted enclosure on the south side, between the two arches that lead into the day chapel. It commemorates Edward Petre (died 1848), a friend of Provost Doyle and a benefactor of St George's. The day chapel is a post-war extension, as is the baptistery to the south of the west door. The carved stone Stations of the Cross were the work of H. J. Youngman. The stained glass in the east window, by Harry Clarke, depicts the Crucifixion and numerous saints and Christian symbols. The same studio designed the west window in 1960, showing the Coronation of the Virgin.

Guy's Hospital Chapel

St Thomas Street

HISTORY
- Built as part of the west wing of the front quadrangle in 1774–7 by Richard Jupp
- The hospital had been founded by Thomas Guy in 1721

OF SPECIAL INTEREST
- Monument to Thomas Guy by John Bacon, 1779 (west wall)
- Mural memorial panels under the galleries
- Memorial to W. E. Gladstone, Prime Minister, a Governor of the hospital
- Stained glass in the east windows, commemorating William Hunt

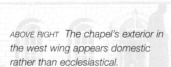

ABOVE RIGHT The chapel's exterior in the west wing appears domestic rather than ecclesiastical.

OPPOSITE John Bacon's distinguished monument to the founder shows Guy helping a patient into his hospital.

The benefaction by which Thomas Guy founded the well-known hospital was one of the largest in London since the Reformation. His monument states that he 'rivalled the endowments of Kings'; for once, an 18th-century eulogy is no exaggeration. He founded his hospital in 1721.

The chapel is the central part of the west wing of the front quadrangle. This wing was added to the designs of Richard Jupp in 1774–7. The interior is almost square and has north and south galleries supported on thin wooden columns with Ionic capitals painted blue. The mural memorial panels of mosaic and opus sectile under the galleries were made by James Powell, 1904. Their dark Edwardian detail stands out in the otherwise light Georgian interior. The sanctuary has a simple marble surround to the arch, by Louis Osman, 1956, in place of a reredos. The stained glass in the windows above commemorates William Hunt (died 1829), the hospital's greatest benefactor after Guy. Against the opposite wall, there stands John Bacon's renowned statue of Guy, made in 1779. It shows the founder helping a suffering man into his hospital, framed by an arch with a green marble surround and enclosed by a semicircular railing. The inscription is paraphrased by the motto on the arms above: 'to give is better than to receive'.

Underneath are deposited the Remains of
THOMAS GUY
Citizen of London Member of Parliament
and the sole Founder of this Hospital
in his Life time

Most Holy Trinity
Dockhead

H.S. Goodhart-Rendel designed this Catholic church, which was built in 1957–60 near Bermondsey's waterfront just downstream of Tower Bridge. It occupies a prominent corner site. The previous church of 1834–5 stood in nearby Parker's Row in a much less conspicuous position; it was destroyed by bombing in 1940.

The interest of the present church is its unusual style, which is markedly different from most contemporary designs, and all the better for that. The focus of interest is undoubtedly the west front of two towers and a huge west window above the main door. The design looks Norman in style and scale, although the details are purely Goodhart-Rendel's. The rest of the church is less striking, but the design throughout is influenced by Norman work. There are patterned brick walls, concrete vaults and a timber roof with slates from Bangor called Welsh greys. The doors have surrounds of green slate from Westmorland. Within, there is the same attention to materials of good quality and decorative inventiveness. The stone panelling in the sanctuary consists of Portland, brown York and blue-grey Forest of Dean stones. Atri Brown was the sculptor. The steps have Belgian marble risers. An African timber called Muninga was used for the floor. A memento of a long-vanished local glory is the mediaeval capital from Bermondsey Abbey, which was found in 1955.

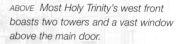

ABOVE Most Holy Trinity's west front boasts two towers and a vast window above the main door.

RIGHT H. S. Goodhart-Rendel paid close attention to the use of high quality materials and decorative inventiveness in this post-war church.

St Barnabas
Calton Avenue

HISTORY
- Built in 1995–6 by Larry Malcic of Helmutt, Obata and Kassabaum to replace a church burnt in 1992
- Rare case of a completely new church in recent years in London

OF SPECIAL INTEREST
- Glass spire
- New pipe organ and case by Kenneth Tickell and Co.
- Patterned stained glass in the east window by Caroline Swash
- The internal plan, with a central altar

ABOVE The thin glass spire can be illuminated and provides a landmark in Dulwich.

RIGHT The church has a central altar, but a major focus is the pairing of the new organ and a stained-glass window at the east end.

St Barnabas's is unusual because it is a fairly lavish new church building of the 1990s, sited within five miles of the centre of London. It was built in 1995–6 by Larry Malcic of the American firm of Helmuth, Obata & Kassabaum to replace a church which had been destroyed by fire in 1992. The modernity of the design ensured that there was determined opposition until planning permission was granted in 1994.

The church stands well back from the road and is attached to ancillary buildings that curve round the right-hand side of the drive. The profile from the west is of two gables of ascending height, and of a tall, thin glass spire beyond. The 19 metre (62 ft) spire attracted disproportionate opposition, given that its shape and size are unexceptional; only its material was novel, and the fact that it could be illuminated. The body of the church is built of russet brick, Cumbrian sandstone and Delabole slate, none of which reflects strident modernity. What is clearly not traditional is the arrangement of the windows, which are very large under the gable ends, but which figure little in the side elevations. The interior might be said to make up an undivided Greek cross at ground level, but there is a longitudinal pull from the wooden roof, which resembles a barrel-vault. The altar is placed in the centre. The more traditional Anglican focus, the east end, now houses the substantial new pipe organ in its decorative case, by Kenneth Tickell & Co., which constitutes the most striking furnishing. It is carefully framed by patterned stained glass in the east window, which Goddard & Gibbs made to the designs of Caroline Swash.

St George the Martyr

Borough High Street

HISTORY

- Built in 1734–6 by John Price on the site of an ancient church
- Known as the 'Little Dorrit church' because it features in Dickens's novel
- Stands at the junction of the Roman Watling and Stane Streets, and the point at which the modern A2 and A3 join

OF SPECIAL INTEREST

- Georgian box-pews, galleries and pulpit
- The organ in the west gallery rebuilt by Abraham Jordan in 1702
- Cherubim on the ceiling, singing the *Te Deum*
- Little Dorrit in the east window

RIGHT St George's has an enviable site at an important road junction.

OPPOSITE The interior preserves its Georgian galleries, box-pews and pulpit. Basil Champneys added the painted plasterwork to the ceiling, showing cherubim singing the Te Deum.

Ghosts of the past teem at the road junction in Borough High Street where St George the Martyr stands in an uncommonly fine position. Roman, mediaeval and modern roads of the first importance have all converged here for 2,000 years. King Henry V, for example, passed by in 1415 after his victory at Agincourt. Dickensian ghosts feature, too: the church is widely known as the Little Dorrit Church, for it features prominently in Dickens's novel of 1857, which was prompted by the imprisonment of the novelist's father as a debtor in the neighbouring Marshalsea Prison in 1824. Little Dorrit appears in the east window, at the bottom right-hand corner. St George's is also notable as the burial-place of Nahum Tate, who wrote the Christmas carol 'While Shepherds watched their Flocks by Night'.

The present church was built in 1734–6 by John Price, in red brick and Portland stone, on the site of a building that had appeared in Hogarth's *Southwark Fair*. The north and south elevations have the usual two tiers of windows to reflect galleries inside, and their brick parapet breaks into a stone balustrade as it nears the west end. The exterior's dominant feature is the west tower, which stands over the main doorway in an eye-catching combination. The fact that the east clock-face of the four in the steeple is not illuminated gave rise to the myth that a snub to Bermondsey was intended. In fact, the original proposal was to light two faces only. A counter-proposal to light all four was then made, and eventually the parish compromised on three. Bermondsey had nothing to do with the matter.

The Georgian interior is well-preserved. It has kept its galleries, of which the west one houses an organ rebuilt by Abraham Jordan in 1702. The box-pews are cut down from the originals, but retain their doors, and the impressive pulpit, held high on four fluted Ionic columns, is one part of the former three-decker. The ceiling is of moulded plaster, which is painted to show cherubim singing the *Te Deum*, originally by Basil Champneys, 1897. Marion Grant designed the postwar stained glass in the east window. There are many old memorials. In the north gallery there are some to the family of Florance Young, a vatmaker whose premises occupied the site of the nearby King's Bench Prison. A brass tablet of 1618 commemorates the wife of a Marshal of the King's Bench, many of whose inmates found their last resting-place in St George's churchyard, some after execution. In 1610 Michael Banks was hanged twice: he revived after the first time and then spent three hours in the vestry before a second and decisive hanging. The church underwent major restoration in 2005–07.

St Giles's Church
Camberwell Church Street

St Giles's Church was built in 1842–4 by Sir George Gilbert Scott to replace a mediaeval building that had been destroyed by fire in 1841. Scott's large new building emphasized Camberwell's transition from country village to prosperous suburb and the change in architectural fashion from Classical to Gothic. Whereas just 20 years earlier the parish had built a daughter-church – St George's, Camberwell – in a monumental Greek Revival style, Sir Gilbert's building was a fully fledged product of the Gothic Revival.

The church was built while Scott was a partner in the firm of Scott & Moffatt. The firm's early fame came from building workhouses for the new Poor Law Unions of the 1830s, but Scott gradually became known for his churches, of which St Giles's was the first important one, and was one of the most significant in the early Gothic Revival. In later years, he immodestly referred to the church in the context of the Gothic Revival as 'the best church by far which had then been erected'. The style is 13th-century Early English, which Scott usually employed (in its later or Geometrical version). The plan is cruciform and includes a crossing tower, with a broach spire rising to 63 metres (207 ft). Scott originally wanted to make the church longer, which would have improved its proportions, but the actual building is still a masterly composition. It is built of Kentish ragstone, with dressings in Caen and Sneaton stone. It was consecrated on 21 November 1844, by the Bishop of Winchester, within whose diocese almost the whole of south London once fell.

The plan is of an aisled nave of five bays, north and south transepts, and a substantial chancel. The present high altar under the crossing dates from 1974. The old chancel is now the Lady chapel. Scott's characteristic gabled reredos at the east end, which now has painted figures in its arches (by Sir Ninian Comper), was originally filled with boards of the Commandments, Lord's Prayer and Creed in the Georgian manner. The interior also differs from its Victorian aspect in lacking the galleries on iron columns which Scott supplied and which were removed after the Second World War. The removal of much

OPPOSITE Sir Gilbert Scott's church of 1842–4 has an east window whose stained glass was designed with John Ruskin's help and on the model of 13th-century French examples.

19th-century glass, together with the church's whitening in 1966, has left a conspicuously light interior. The piers of the nave are alternately round and octagonal. The nave, chancel and transepts have high-pitched roofs; the north porch and the crossing are groined.

Original to Scott's church are the pews, pulpit and organ case, supplied by Samuel Pratt of New Bond Street. The choirstalls came from Lady Margaret Church in Walworth. J. C. Bishop supplied the organ, designed by Samuel Sebastian Wesley, the well-known 19th-century musician, who was organist here in 1829–32. He was the great-nephew of John Wesley. As it happens, Mary Wesley, John's wife, is buried here. She died in 1781.

The 14th-century sedilia and piscina are from the old church and were placed in the present building only in 1916. The eight brasses on the south wall of the south transept, which date from between 1492 and 1637, were also rescued from old St Giles's. Among other memorials, is one on the south transept's west wall to the First Surrey Rifles, which was removed from the regimental depot in Flodden Road in 1962. The icon in the south transept was given in 1980 by the local Greek Orthodox congregation, which worshipped in St Giles's for some years. In the north aisle there is a memorial by Eric Gill to Charles Frederick Gurney Masterman (died 1927), the Liberal politician and reformer, who lived in Camberwell. In the opposite aisle a marble tablet commemorates Captain Nairne, who served the Honourable East India Company, was a director of the shipping firm, P. & O., and fought under Nelson at the Battle of Copenhagen in 1801.

The great east window was made by the firm of Ward & Nixon and was pieced together in 1950 after being shattered in the Second World War. It is often stated that the window was designed by John Ruskin, who was a parishioner, although Ruskin's autobiography states clearly that he gave way in the matter to his friend, Edmund Oldfield. Ruskin certainly studied French stained glass (as he put it, 'the tracery of the east window seemed to us convertible into no dishonouring likeness of something at Rheims or Chartres'), but Oldfield was evidently just as learned. The window follows the 13th-century French style and comprises rich purple and red medallions. The central light depicts the Nativity, Temptation, Crucifixion, Resurrection and Ascension. The two lights to the left show Old Testament scenes; the two to the right illustrate the Acts of the Apostles. Our Lord's baptism and the Last Supper appear in the tracery lights.

The west window contains 13th-century glass from Trier. Acquired at the time of rebuilding, it was repaired by Ward & Nixon. Sir Ninian Comper designed two windows in the south transept. The one above the brasses, installed in 1956, depicts St Giles with the deer. The 10th-century legend (three centuries after the saint's actual life) states that a King Wamba shot at a deer which Giles was protecting, but crippled Giles instead. Hence the saint's later fame as a patron of cripples. All that is really known of St Giles is that he was a 7th-century hermit in Provence.

St Mary's Rotherhithe
St Marychurch Street

ABOVE Four giant columns divide the interior, which preserves much of its 18th-century atmosphere, despite Victorian alterations.

OPPOSITE Lancelot Dowbiggin's tower and steeple were added in 1747–8 to John James's church of 1714–15.

St Mary's has a notable part in the story of the *Mayflower*, which took the Pilgrim Fathers to North America in 1620, for its master, Christopher Jones, lies buried there. He is not the only reminder of Rotherhithe's maritime past. Among the memorials there is one to Captain Anthony Wood, Jones's contemporary, which features a fine carving of a ship. On the south wall there is a memorial to Joseph Wade (died 1743), King's Carver at Deptford. In the 18th and 19th centuries, many ships were built at Rotherhithe for the Royal Navy and many were eventually broken up there. These included the *Temeraire*, which Turner famously painted. Chairs made from the *Temeraire*'s timbers are kept in the church.

St Mary's stands in a narrow street near the Thames, opposite a charity school of about 1700 and the rectory, and amidst old warehouses. It has a tall, balustraded west tower of red brick with stone quoins, which is surmounted by an open circular stage of Corinthian columns and a short spire. Lancelot Dowbiggin added this tower in 1747–8, to a church John James had rebuilt in 1714–15.

The interior is divided by four tall Ionic columns into three unequal bays. Their panelled bases speak of the box-pews that once filled the church. The west gallery houses a celebrated organ built by John Byfield the younger in 1764–5. At the east end, there is the original reredos, carved by Joseph Wade. Above, 16th-century German glass depicts the Assumption.

A brass in the north aisle commemorates Peter Hills (died 1614), who founded the charity school. Lee Boo (died 1784), a prince from the Pacific island of Belau, has a tomb that is inscribed: 'Stop reader, stop! let Nature claim a tear/A Prince of mine, Lee Boo, lies buried here'.

Christ Church
Commercial Street

RIGHT Giant columns divide Hawksmoor's interior, seen here in 1999 before restoration.

Spitalfields was in ancient times part of the huge parish of St Dunstan, Stepney, which stretched from the City to Bow and from Hackney to the Thames. It now has a vividly Asian colour, largely Bangladeshi. London's suburban development in this direction began early, and already in the Middle Ages the hamlets of Whitechapel and Bow were given churches of their own. In the 17th century the pace of development increased and the hamlets of Wapping, Shadwell and Poplar were separated ecclesiastically. The Fifty New Churches Act gave the ancient parish three more churches: at Limehouse (St Anne's), at Upper Wapping (St George's in the East) and at Spitalfields (Christ Church). All three were designed by Nicholas Hawksmoor and rank among the most important churches in London.

Within two months of the appointment of Commissioners under the Act of 1711, it was decided that Spitalfields should have two new churches. This was in the heady days when 50 churches really were envisaged, and no fewer than five were listed for Stepney. Opposition soon came from Sir George Wheler, proprietor of the Wheler Chapel, who feared that a new church in Norton Folgate (just north of Liverpool Street Station) would damage his interest. The other proposal for the district, for Christ Church, was unopposed but progressed slowly. A site was bought in 1713. On 9 April 1714 Hawksmoor submitted a design, which was duly approved. It was not the design for the whole building we see today, and its estimated cost was only a fraction of the £40,000 eventually needed.

Foundations were dug in mid-1714 and work proceeded until the church was consecrated in 1729. As in so many of the Commissioners' works, progress was initially good and was then curtailed, for by about 1719 debts threatened the entire series of churches. As late as 1727, an important decision was made: the Commissioners ordered that the spire was to be built according to a design sent in by Hawksmoor. This was a major part of the eventual building and was not approved until the very end of the works.

An Act passed in 1729 created a new parish of Spitalfields and provided the sum of £3,000 to endow the living, but leaving the parish the task of raising £125 a year through local rates. The church was consecrated by the Bishop of London on 5 July 1729. One of the Commissioners, Edward Peck, lived locally. He had laid the foundation stone in 1715 and was rewarded at the church's completion by being given a private pew and a burial vault. When he died in 1736, a monument was erected here, to the design of Thomas Dunn. It is not often that an 'ordinary' Commissioner, as opposed to such people as Sir Isaac Newton and Sir Robert Walpole, can be identified in a memorial.

The exterior is dominated by the west tower and spire, which face down Brushfield Street. The tower is an extraordinary one among London's churches. At its base there is a huge portico, comprising four soaring Tuscan columns, whose spacing is wider in the centre than at the sides. Each lateral pair of

columns supports a straight entablature. A central arch then rises above and connects the whole. The next stage up is square, with another central arch rising above its associated features. Finally, there comes a broach spire, rising to 68.6 metres (225 ft), which Sir John Summerson described as a paraphrase of St Mary's, Stamford. Until 1822 this spire had openings and crockets: it was a little more Gothic. There should be nothing too surprising about Hawksmoor's Gothic essay, for he designed the west towers of Westminster Abbey, which are among the most familiar Gothic landmarks of London. What is striking about Christ Church's tower is its apparent substantial width when seen from the west. This is achieved by deep buttressing.

The interior seems more longitudinal than one sees in Hawksmoor's churches. His usual central square is not obvious. A central square does exist in Christ Church, but it is not so apparent here as elsewhere. Tall columns carry block entablatures, which are returned to the aisle walls. Each aisle bay has a transverse barrel-vault. The nave has a clerestory and a flat ceiling. The reinstated galleries are visually important. There were also box-pews, the absence of which make the tall bases of the columns look rather odd. You cannot judge a Georgian interior without envisaging the whole original ensemble. Towards the east end the entablature is carried across the church on two columns, acting the part of an extraordinary chancel screen. Above, there are the royal arms in stone. To the east, there are quadrant walls to frame the altar recess, which is dominated by a large Venetian window. It contains

stained glass depicting the Annunciation and Christ's childhood (left); the Last Supper and the Ascension (centre); and Baptism, Transfiguration and Calvary (right). The west gallery houses an organ by Richard Bridges, 1735. Near the west door there are memorials that came from the Episcopal Jews' Chapel in Bethnal Green when it was demolished in 1895.

Christ Church had to be closed in 1958 when the roof was found to be unsafe. Ever since, restoration has been planned or carried out, to strengthen the fabric and to put back the Georgian ensemble. Worship resumed here in 1987.

St Anne's Church

Commercial Road

HISTORY

- Built in 1714–24 by Nicholas Hawksmoor
- One of the Fifty New Churches
- Restoration carried out by Philip Hardwick and John Morris after a fire in 1850
- Greatly restored and cleaned in recent years

OF SPECIAL INTEREST

- West steeple
- Stained glass in the east window by Charles Clutterbuck
- Hawksmoor's plan based on four giant columns

ABOVE One of the four columns that divide the interior.

OPPOSITE The west steeple is Hawksmoor's version of a 15th-century lantern tower and was for many years a famous landmark for mariners on the Thames.

Limehouse was a hamlet in the parish of St Dunstan, Stepney, when it was first judged worthy of having its own church in the early 18th century. Within a hundred years, the view from the tower of St Anne's would encompass a scene of intense maritime activity, including the great shipbuilding yards of the Thames, where scores of East Indiamen, ships of the Royal Navy and merchant vessels were built and refitted. Today, the tall masts are long since gone, and the same view from St Anne's encompasses Canary Wharf, whose monumental tower dwarfs anything from an earlier age.

The church was built to Nicholas Hawksmoor's designs in 1714–24, under the Fifty New Churches Act. It was the only one of the churches built under that Act – 'the Queen Anne Act' – that was named in allusion to the reigning monarch. Her popular standing in the Church derived very largely from her foundation of Queen Anne's Bounty, which was a re-direction of ancient ecclesiastical revenues to add to parochial endowments. It was merged into the work of the Church Commissioners in 1948. The first moves to build St Anne's were made in late 1711; the new church came into use only in 1730. Progress in building was slow. The foundations were laid by November 1714, but the church was not completed until 1724. The total cost of the building was over £32,000. The church remained unused for some six years, on account of insufficient funds to support a priest (for the Commissioners had too little money to provide an immediate endowment). When the first rector, Robert Leybourne, was eventually installed in September 1729, he held the parish together with that of St Dunstan until 1759. The church came into use in 1730 and the registers survive from that date.

The tower is Hawksmoor's version of a 15th-century example with a lantern. Projecting buttresses to north and south make it seem wider from the west. On that side there is the original main doorway within a semicircular projection. The vestibules to left and right have attics. In the upper part of the tower there are two stages set diagonally against each other: a typical Baroque arrangement. The north and south

elevations are relatively plain, with two tiers of windows, usual for an 18th-century church, to reflect the galleries within. At the eastern angles there are square turrets. A drawing in the British Library suggests that these turrets were meant to be surmounted by pyramids. It is possible that the unusual pyramidal tomb in the churchyard might have had something to do with that plan. The exterior's gleaming Portland stone was restored and cleaned in 1985–90 by grant of the London Docklands Development Corporation.

The interior is centred on Hawksmoor's stock-in-trade of a square within a square. The tall nave is divided by four columns into an inner square, two 'transepts' and east and west arms. All the arms of the cross are of equal height. To the east there is a projecting rectangular sanctuary; to the west there is one additional bay. Thus the centralizing Greek cross is pulled somewhat into the longitudinal plan of mediaeval convention. There are north, south and west galleries.

On Good Friday, 1850, a fire damaged the interior and destroyed the fittings. Restoration was carried out by Philip Hardwick and John Morris. The work followed the original style and made no attempt to Gothicize the church.

The new font was Hardwick's; the oak pulpit was carved by William Gibbs Rogers – one of the best Victorian carvers in London – to the designs of the young Arthur Blomfield, who was Hardwick's pupil. In 1891 Blomfield was to be called in again to undertake further works, chiefly the introduction of choir-stalls. The huge east window is filled with the Crucifixion in coloured enamels on white glass, by Charles Clutterbuck. It suits the setting very well but the enamel paint was badly fired. Clutterbuck was successful when he adopted a pictorial manner rather than a more mediaeval approach. The replacement organ was by Gray and Davidson. One memorial, to William Curling (died 1853), who is descibed as 'an eminent shipbuilder of this parish', is a reminder of the days when the Thames was a great centre of shipbuilding. Just five years after Curling's death, the biggest ship of the Victorian world, the *Great Eastern,* was launched a little downstream of Limehouse.

LEFT Despite a fire in 1850 and Victorian restorations, St Anne's has retained its galleries. After years of decline, the church has lately seen considerable repair and revival.

RIGHT Galleries provided much-needed additional seating in Georgian churches, and staircases were normally placed in the corners of a church to reach them.

BELOW A view at gallery level towards the organ at the west end.

St John's Chapel
White Tower, Tower of London

HISTORY
- The oldest Norman church in London
- Built in the late 11th century when the White Tower was built as the keep of William the Conqueror's fortress
- Derives its character from its heavy, monumental architecture

OF SPECIAL INTEREST
- Vistas made by the piers and arches
- The designs of the capitals: scallops, leaves and volutes

The White Tower is the oldest part of William the Conqueror's fortress. It was built between about 1077 and 1097 as the keep or citadel. St John's Chapel on the second floor is an impressive and complete survival from *early* in the Norman period, unlike many other Norman churches in England which date from the mid-12th century.

It consists of a tunnel-vaulted nave, with an east apse, and groin-vaulted aisles with a tunnel-vaulted gallery above, which curve round the apse, as at St Bartholomew the Great, Smithfield. Thick, round piers support unmoulded arches. The only adornment is the carving of the capitals which consists largely of simple scallop and leaf designs and, in one case, volutes. The piers of the gallery are square and stand directly above those of the lower arcade. The whole impresses by its proportions and its strength. It certainly deserves to be better known among London's historic churches.

ABOVE An ambulatory runs round the chapel, affording changing vistas of arches and columns.

RIGHT A gaunt solemnity is imparted by the ponderous features of the chapel in William the Conqueror's 11th-century keep.

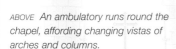

154

St Peter ad Vincula

Tower Green, Tower of London

ABOVE The two Tudor Lieutenants of the Tower commemorated here, Sir Richard Blount and his son, Sir Michael, would have witnessed many of the scenes that prompted Thomas Macaulay to say 'there is no sadder place on earth'.

ABOVE RIGHT St Peter's from Tower Green: the four-centred arches of the windows are typical of Tudor design.

The chapel's name refers to St Peter's first imprisonment under Herod in Jerusalem and translates as 'St Peter in chains'. Although the Tower has existed since the time of William the Conqueror, most people think of it in connection with the Tudors, especially with King Henry VIII. It is appropriate, therefore, that the Chapel Royal of St Peter ad Vincula, the Tower's parish church, should date from his reign: the present building was completed in 1520. St Peter's stands north of Tower Green, where executions took place, and so many famous victims of the block and axe were buried in the adjoining church. Queen Anne Boleyn and Queen Catherine Howard, the second and fifth wives of King Henry VIII, Lady Jane Grey and St Thomas More and St John Fisher, who became saints of the Catholic Church, all found a resting place there.

The chapel consists of a nave and a shorter north aisle. The windows have cusped lights but no tracery: a common feature of late mediaeval Gothic. A diminutive, quoined tower, surmounted by a lantern bell-cote, stands at the west end. The chief features are the monuments. A substantial one, which stands in the sanctuary, commemorates Sir Richard Blount (died 1564; right) and his son, Sir Michael (died 1596), Lieutenants of the Tower. The kneeling figures are enclosed within arches supported by Corinthian columns. Another Lieutenant, Sir Richard Cholmondeley (died 1544), lies in effigy under the central arcade. Finally, in the north-west corner, a large monument commemorates John Holland, Duke of Exeter (died 1447), Constable of the Tower.

Addresses and Directions

1 All Hallows by the Tower: Byward Street, EC3R 5BJ; immediately west of the Tower of London. 020 7481 2928, www.ahbtt.org.uk

2 All Hallows on the Wall: 83 London Wall, EC2M 5ND; on the north side of London Wall, near Liverpool Street Station. 020 7588 2638, www.allhallowsonthewall.org

3 All Saints: Margaret Street, W1W 8JG; north-east of Oxford Circus, off Regent Street. 020 7636 1788, www.allsaintsmargaretstreet.org.uk

4 Christ Church: Commercial Street, E1 6LY; on the corner of Fournier Street and opposite the junction with Brushfield Street. Church office: 020 7377 2440, www.ccspitalfields.org

5 Farm Street Church: 114 Mount Street, W1K 3AH; in Mount Street, Mayfair, opposite the Connaught Hotel and a little south of Grosvenor Square; Parish priest: 020 7493 7811, www.farmstreet.org.uk

6 Guy's Hospital Chapel: St Thomas Street, SE1; on the west side of the front quadrangle of Guy's Hospital, just by London Bridge Station. 020 7188 5588, www.guysandthomas.nhs.uk

7 London Oratory: Brompton Road, SW7 2RP; at the junction of Brompton Road and Cromwell Road in South Kensington, between Harrod's and the Victoria and Albert Museum. 020 7808 0900, www.bromptonoratory.com

8 Most Holy Trinity: Priest's House, Dockhead, SE1 2BS; at the western end of Jamaica Road, just east of the south end of Tower Bridge. 020 7237 1641, www.dockhead.com

9 Old Royal Naval College Chapel: King William Walk, SE10 9LW, part of the grand buildings fronting the Thames. General enquiries: 020 8269 4747, www.oldroyalnaval college.org

10 Southwark Cathedral: London Bridge, SE1 9DA; just upstream of London Bridge on the south side, opposite London Bridge Station. 020 7367 6700, www.cathedral. southwark.anglican.org

11 St Alfege: Greenwich Church Street, SE10 9BJ; in Greenwich Church Street, where the road curves round to become Greenwich High Road – the west end of Greenwich's centre. Church office: 020 8853 0687, www.st-alfege.org

12 St Anne's Church: Commercial Road, Limehouse, E14 7HP; situated on the main east-west road along the river. 020 7987 1502

13 St Augustine: Kilburn Park Road, NW6; between Harrow Road and Maida Vale. Parish priest: 020 7624 1637, www.saint-augustine.org.uk

14 St Barnabas: 38 Calton Avenue, SE21; situated off Dulwich Village. Parish office: 020 8693 1524, www.stbarnabasdulwich.org

15 St Bartholomew the Great: West Smithfield, EC1; between St Bartholomew's Hospital and Smithfield Market. 020 7606 5171, www.great stbarts.com

16 St Bride's Fleet Street: Fleet Street, EC4Y 8AU; south side of Fleet Street, near Ludgate Circus. 020 7427 0133, www.stbrides.com

17 St Clement Danes: Strand, WC2R 1DH; in the middle of the road at the east end of the Strand (where it is about to become Fleet Street), opposite the Law Courts. 020 7242 8282, www.raf.mod.uk/ stclementdanes/

18 St Cyprian's: Glentworth Street, NW1 6AX; near the entrance to Regent's Park at the very north end of Baker Street. Administrator: 020 7258 0724, www.stcyprians.org.uk

19 St Etheldreda's: Ely Place, EC1N 6RY; in a cul-de-sac off Charterhouse Street, just after it leaves Holborn Circus. 020 7405 1061, www.stethelreda.com

20 St George the Martyr: Borough High Street, SE1 1JA; at the junction with Long Lane, opposite Borough Underground Station, just south of London Bridge. 020 7537 7331, www.stgeorge-the martyr.co.uk

21 St George's: St George Street, W1; at the junction of St George's Street with Maddox Street, just south of Hanover Square. 020 7629 0874, www.stgeorges hanoversquare.org

22 St George's Bloomsbury: Bloomsbury Way, WC1A 2HR; in Bloomsbury Way, a few yards east of its junction with Museum Street (which leads through to the British Museum), just off New Oxford Street. 020 7242 1979, www.stgeorges bloomsbury.org.uk

23 St George's Cathedral: Lambeth Road, SE1 7HY; situated at the junction of Lambeth Road and St George's Road. Administrator: 020 7928 5256, www.southwark-rc-cathedral.org.uk

24 St Giles Church: Camberwell Church Street, SE5; a few hundred yards east of Camberwell Green. Vicar: 020 7703 4504, www.stgiles camberwell.org.uk

25 St Helen's Bishopsgate: Great St Helen's, EC3A 6AT; off Bishopsgate, just south of Liverpool Street Station. 020 7283 2231, www.st-helens-org.uk

26 St John's Chapel: White Tower, Tower of London EC3; chapel within the White Tower (the keep). www.hrp.org.uk

27 St Katharine Cree: Leadenhall Street, EC3; in Leadenhall Street, near Lloyd's and Aldgate. Church manager: 020 7488 4318, www.sanctuaryinthecity.net

28 St Magnus the Martyr: Lower Thames Street, EC3R 6DN; just downstream of London Bridge at the northern end. Office: 020 7626 4481, www.stmagnus martyr.org.uk

29 St Margaret's Church: St Margaret Street, SW1P 3JX; on south side of Parliament Square, in front of the north-east corner of Westminster Abbey, St Margaret's is run in tandem with Westminster Abbey. 020 7654 4840, www.westminster-abbey.org/st-margarets

30 St Martin-in-the-Fields: Trafalgar Square, WC2N 4JJ; north-east corner of Trafalgar Square, at the beginning of St Martin's Lane. 020 7766 1100, www2.stmartin-in-the-fields.org

31 St Mary Abbots: Kensington Church Street, W8; stands at the junction with Kensington High Street. 020 7937 2419, www.stmaryabbots church.org

32 St Mary-at-Lambeth: Lambeth Palace Road, SE1 7LB; sited at the south end of Lambeth Bridge, near St Thomas's Hospital, now forms the premises of the Garden Museum. 020 7401 8865, www.gardenmuseum.org.uk

33 St Mary's Rotherhithe: St Marychurch Street, SE16; near Rotherhithe Tunnel's entrance at the eastern end of Jamaica Road. www.stmaryrotherhithe.org

34 St Mary-le-Bow: Cheapside, EC2V 6AU. 020 7248 5139, www.stmarylebow.co.uk

35 St Nicholas's: Deptford Green, SE8 3DQ; off the main road between Rotherhithe and Greenwich. 020 8692 2749, www.deptfordchurch.org

36 St Pancras Parish Church: Upper Woburn Place, WC1; at the corner of Euston Road and Upper Woburn Place, opposite the fire station and diagonally opposite Euston Station. 020 7388 1461, www.stpancraschurch.org

37 St Paul's Cathedral: Ludgate Hill, EC4M 8AD; at the top of Ludgate Hill. 020 7236 4128, www.stpauls.co.uk

38 St Paul's Church: Bedford Street, WC2E 9ED; situated on the west side of Covent Garden, but entered from the other end (in Bedford Street). Rector: 020 7836 5221, www.actorschurch.org

39 St Paul's Church: Diamond Way, Deptford SE8 3DS; off Deptford High Street. 020 8692 0989, www.paulsdeptford.org.uk

40 St Peter ad Vincula: Tower Green, Tower of London, EC3; chapel within the Tower of London, on Tower Green. www.hrp.org.uk

41 St Stephen Walbrook: 39 Walbrook, EC4N 8BN; situated behind the Mansion House, which looks onto the Bank Station junction. 020 7626 9000, www.ststephenwalbrook.net/

42 Temple Church: Fleet Street, EC4Y 7BB; situated just south of Fleet Street, opposite Chancery Lane. Church visits and bookings: 020 7353 3470, www.temple church.com

43 Wesley's Chapel: Wesley's Chapel and Leysian Mission, 49 City Road, EC1Y 1AU; in City Road, just north of the City. 020 7253 2262, www.wesleys chapel.org.uk

44 Westminster Abbey: Parliament Square, SW1. Chapter Office: 020 7222 5152, www.westminster-abbey.org/

45 Westminster Cathedral: Francis Street, SW1P 1QW; off Victoria Street, near Victoria Station. 020 7798 9055, www.westminstercathedral.org.uk

46 Westminster Methodist Central Hall: Storey's Gate, Westminster, SW1H 9NH; opposite Westminster Abbey. Church office: 020 7654 3809, www.methodist-central-hall.org.uk

47 Westminster, St John's: Smith Square, SW1; off Millbank, near the Houses of Parliament. Administrator: 020 7222 2168, www.sjss.org.uk

Glossary

Abbey A monastery under the control of an abbot.

Ambulatory A processional way round the east end of a larger church, beyond the high altar and connecting with the chancel aisles.

Apse A rounded or polygonal termination to a church, usually at the east end of the chancel, sometimes at the east end of a chapel or aisle, but very rarely at the west end.

Benedictine Relating to the order of monks whose rule was devised by St Benedict of Nursia (died about 550).

Box-pew A high, enclosed pew, normal in English churches from the 17th to the 19th century.

Canon A priest who has an official position in a cathedral or a collegiate church, either full-time or honorary. In some mediaeval monasteries, such as Southwark Cathedral and St Bartholomew the Great, Smithfield, the monks were termed canons.

Canted At an angle.

Capital The decorative capping of a column or pilaster.

Cathedra The chair or throne of a bishop, which gives its name to his cathedral. In Classical times, a special chair was the symbol of a teacher's authority; a bishop is meant to teach the Christian Faith authoritatively.

Chancel The east part of a church, which normally houses the high altar and is generally the preserve of the clergy and choir.

Chantry A special chapel set aside for prayers and services for the soul of someone who has died, or the endowment to support it. (*See* St George's Cathedral.)

Choir Either a body of singers, or the east part of a church, in which they sing. The choir of a church is normally part of its chancel.

Clerestory The 'clear storey' or row of windows at a high level to give light to a church, usually above a nave but sometimes above the chancel as well.

Coffering Decoration on a vault or on the soffit of an arch in the form of sunken panels.

Collegiate Of or concerning a college: either a college of priests (e.g. Westminster Abbey) or a university college, in whose chapel the seats will often face north and south, not east.

Crossing The part of a cruciform church where the four arms join.

Cruciform Shaped like a cross. A Greek cross has arms of equal length; a Latin cross has one arm longer than the remaining three.

Cusp A pointed shape formed in tracery, where two foils meet.

Dean The usual title of the priest who is in charge of a cathedral (e.g. St Paul's Cathedral) or a collegiate church (e.g. Westminster Abbey).

Decorated The architectural style predominant in the early 14th century, in which curvilinear forms became the most obvious features.

Dog-tooth A form of moulding or carved decoration - characteristic of the 13th century.

Domesday Book A survey of England compiled in 1086 by order of William the Conqueror. It mentions many churches for the first time.

Early English The architectural style normal in England in the 13th century: the first Gothic style.

Easter Sepulchre A tomb or tomb-like structure on the north side of a sanctuary, which serves to shelter the Reserved Sacrament between Maundy Thursday and Easter Sunday, in allusion to Christ's burial in the Holy Sepulchre.

Entablature The horizontal superstructure resting on columns or pilasters. A *block entablature* rests on a single column and does not run straight across to the next column.

Fluted Vertical concave lines on a pillar or pilaster, common in Classical buildings.

Gothic The style of the pointed arch, starting in England in the 12th century and lasting until the 17th; it was then consciously revived and as a revived style had its heyday in Victorian times.

Great Fire Took place in September 1666, and burnt about four-fifths of the City of London.

Groin-vault A vault formed by two tunnel-vaults joining at right angles.

Hexastyle Sixfold, as in a portico with six columns.

Lady chapel A chapel named in honour of the Virgin Mary. In smaller churches, it would be found at the east end of an aisle, or north or south of the chancel. In very large churches, it would often be east of the high altar.

Lancet Tall, thin, single-light window, undivided by mullions or tracery. Most typical of the 13th century, but occurs in smaller form in Norman churches.

Light The vertical division of a window.

Minster In England before Norman times, a church that was more ancient or important than its neighbours. The name comes from the Latin *monasterium*, but it was not necessarily a monastery.

Nave The west part of a church, in which the greater part of the congregation sits. A *nave altar* is an altar placed at the east end of a nave, rather than at the east end of the chancel; it may be fixed or movable.

Pediment In Classical architecture, a triangular capping to a façade or portico. Sometimes the lower side is deliberately left incomplete or 'broken', or the upper sides do not meet at the apex.

Pelican in her piety A carving of a pelican biting her breast, to symbolize self-sacrifice and so to allude to the Eucharist.

Perpendicular The architectural style predominant between the late 14th and early 16th centuries, in which perpendicular panels in window tracery are characteristic.

Pilaster A flat pillar fixed to a wall and possessing the base and capital of a Classical order.

Piscina Bowl or stoup with a drain and (usually) an ornamented canopy that is placed in the south wall of a chancel for the ritual washing of the chalice and other vessels. It is a feature of mediaeval churches and also of Victorian ones.

Priory A monastery under the control of a prior.

Provost The title of the priest who runs a cathedral that is also a parish church, e.g. Southwark Cathedral.

Pyx A container for the Reserved Sacrament, which was often suspended above the high altar in mediaeval churches and is used in some modern churches (*see* All Saints, Margaret Street).

Quadrant A quarter of a circle.

Rector The title given in the Middle Ages to the individual to whom the whole income of a church was due. Today, the titles of 'rector' and 'vicar' do not normally have practical distinctions.

Reformation The movement in the 16th century in which the authority of the Pope was repudiated and new interpretations of Scripture took hold. In England, it started under King Henry VIII but went much further under King Edward VI.

Reliquary A container for relics of a saint.

Reredos An altarpiece: a wooden or stone structure standing behind, and giving honour to, an altar, usually adorned with paintings or sculpture.

Retrochoir Literally, 'at the back of the choir'; in larger churches, an area to the east of the high altar, usually including one or more chapels (*see* Southwark Cathedral).

Rood A crucifix placed above a chancel screen or sometimes suspended from the roof, flanked by the Virgin Mary and St John, and occasionally by angels.

Sanctuary The east end of a chancel, in which the high altar stands, often marked out by communion rails or a step.

Sedilia Seats for the clergy, usually in threes, and placed on the south side of the sanctuary.

Tester A canopy over a pulpit (also called a sounding-board) and sometimes over another furnishing.

Three-decker pulpit Between the 17th and 19th centuries, many churches had a pulpit of three tiers or decks, of which the top one was the pulpit proper, for preaching; the middle one was a reading-desk; and below was the clerk's pew.

Tractarian Originally, one who supported the views of *Tracts for the Times*, which were religious pamphlets of the 1830s and early 1840s; later, anyone with High Church or Anglo-Catholic views.

Transept A lateral part of a church, usually extending north and/or south of the crossing or of the east part of the nave.

Tree of Jesse A family tree to show Christ's descent from Jesse via St Joseph.

Triptych Threefold. Normally used of a painting divided into three folding panels, which is used as a reredos.

Tunnel-vault A semicircular or cylindrical vault.

Tympanum The space enclosed by a pediment or the space between a door's lintel and an arch above it. Such spaces are often filled with carving.

Venetian window In Classical buildings, a window in which a large arched light is flanked by lower, straight-topped lights.

Vicar From the Latin, *vicarius*, a substitute. Originally, a priest who took the place of a rector. There is now no practical distinction between a vicar and a rector.

This edition published in 2011 by
New Holland Publishers (UK) Ltd
London • Cape Town • Sydney • Auckland

10 9 8 7 6 5 4 3 2 1

www.newhollandpublishers.com

Garfield House, 86–88 Edgware Road,
London W2 2EA, United Kingdom

80 McKenzie Street, Cape Town 8001, South Africa

Unit 1, 66 Gibbes Street, Chatswood, NSW 2067, Australia

218 Lake Road, Northcote, Auckland, New Zealand

All the photographs in this book were taken by James
Morris, except the front cover photograph of St Paul's
Cathedral © Pixtal Images/Photolibrary.

Cover and Preliminary Pages Photographs:
Front cover: St Paul's Cathedral (top), Westminster
Abbey (bottom); Spine: St Augustine, Kilburn; Back
cover: St Martin-in-the-Fields; Half title: Mediaeval choir
at St Bartholomew's Priory Church, Smithfield; p.2: the
east portico of St Paul's, Covent Garden; p.6: ceiling
detail St Martin-in-the-Fields; p.7: Organ, Chapel of the
Former Royal Naval College, Greenwich.

ISBN 978 1 84773 802 8

Publisher: Guy Hobbs
Designer & Cover Design: Isobel Gillan
Production: Marion Storz
Cartography: Stephen Dew

Reproduction by Pica Digital (Pte) Ltd, Singapore
Printed and bound in Singapore by
   Tien Wah Press Pte Ltd

Acknowledgements

AUTHOR: As you study churches all over this country,
you appreciate the context of particular features on your
doorstep. The writer on churches cannot afford to be
parochial. This particular group of buildings has reintro-
duced me to many old friends and has made me look at
them anew. In particular, it has taken me back to Wren's
City of London churches, where I first began to study
churches seriously forty years ago. The example of the
late Dr Gordon Huelin at St Margaret Pattens was an
important one to me, and properly finds a mention here.

   I also gladly record my thanks to the Reverend
Anthony Yates, Vicar of St Augustine's, Kilburn, for his
kindness in admitting me to the church and in explaining
various features. Acknowledgement is also made to the
writings of the late Reverend Basil Clarke, which taught
the value of archival sources and the importance of the
context of a building in church history.

Stephen Humphrey

PHOTOGRAPHER: In photographing these churches I
had to ask the co-operation of too many people to
mention here. Most were very accommodating, and
some charming and welcoming. I thank them all.
Undertaking the photography was a great chance to
explore some of London's most wonderful buildings. The
most fascinating were usually the least visited;
Hawksmoor's St Anne's Limehouse is wonderful in its
state of decaying grandeur, likewise Christ Church
Spitalfields. St George's Bloomsbury is the perfect 18th
century urban church, though easy to miss. St John's
Chapel in the Tower of London retains its simple Norman
purity like no other in London. St Augustine's was
unknown to me and a great discovery, a vast Gothic
extravagance in the heart of Kilburn. Most of these
churches hold surprises. I was privileged to be able to
explore these buildings without restriction, and I hope
they can become equally accessible to all.

James Morris